# BAREFOOT,

# NAKED,

# AND IN THE KITCHEN

Sweet, Sassy, and Sanctified: Reignighting a Holy Fire in a Culture that Can't Light a Match.

## By: Holly T. Ashley

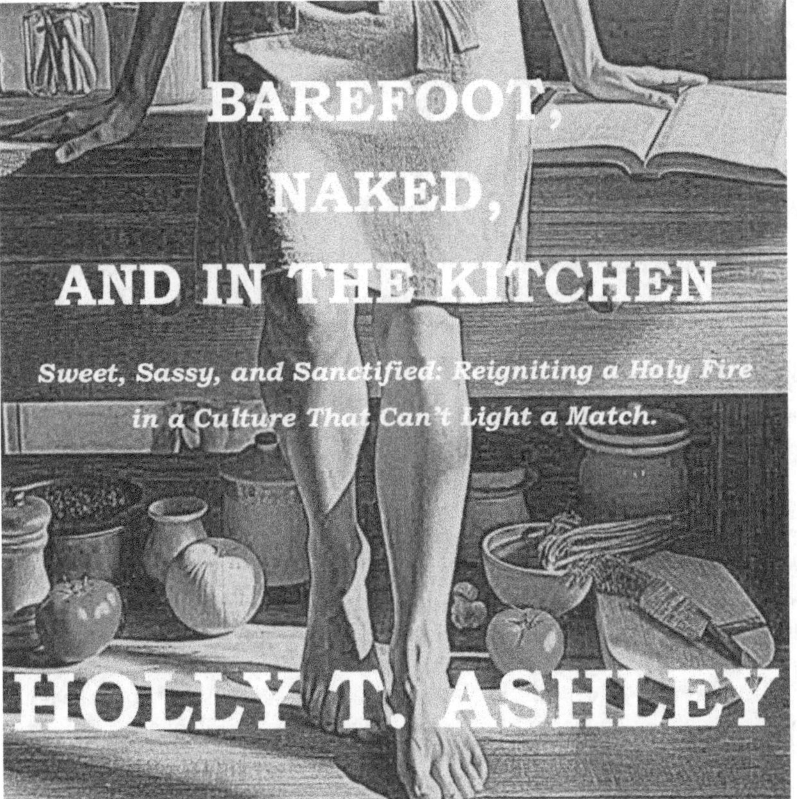

BAREFOOT,
NAKED,
AND IN THE KITCHEN
Sweet, Sassy, and Sanctified: Reigniting a Holy Fire
in a Culture That Can't Light a Match.
HOLLY T. ASHLEY

# COPYRIGHT

*Barefoot Naked and in the Kitchen Sweet, Sassy, and Sanctified: Reigniting Holy Fire in a Culture That Can't Light a Match*
*By: Holly T. Ashley*

# Dedication

**To my beloved husband, David Ashley — "The Pastor of Pump"**

My patient, ever-loving, immovable, strong man. Strong biblically. Strong emotionally. Strong lovingly. Strong physically. Thank you for weathering my mood swings, hormone swings, libido swings, and every other sanctification curveball the Lord has seen fit to throw my way. Thank you for loving me with steadiness when I'm fiery, faithful, fragile, and occasionally feral.

You lead with conviction, cover me with grace, and love me in a way that makes the gospel visible. I am grateful for you— Thank you for constantly reminding me that Jesus carries me. And I am grateful that somehow, by His mercy, you keep up. I love you desperately.

**And to my Tribe—**

**Dagney (DJ), Melissa, Jen, Hali, Gwen, Kelly, and Rayna.**

We laugh at the fact that we cry. We cry because life is holy, hard, and wildly inconvenient. We laugh again because if we don't, we'd probably get kicked out of church. You cheer, you hold me accountable, you pray, you show up, and we cry or laugh some more— usually in that exact order. Thank you for being the kind of friend who tell the truth, pass the tissues, and never flinch when things get real. I love you fiercely.

*If you don't have honest friends – You have no friends at all.*

-Holly T. Ashley

# Preface

David and I have heard all the jokes, the remarks, the whispers, the giggles… I see the "gag me" posts on social media and the raise eyebrows of those who have yet to discover "David and Holly Ashley." But the truth is – We are not the norm. We do not fight, we do not argue, we do not embarrass each other in public or act unloving or unkind to one another. We do disagree – but we maintain honor and respect towards one another. But again, we are much older, wiser, now – and I can tell you by knowing my own personality and through my experiences with myself and others, that this would not have been the case had we gotten married forty years ago, as we had planned…

But more about that later.

David and I are indeed different from most. What you see is exactly what you get – whether we are in public or behind closed doors. I never open doors; I don't pay for meals (although I am the keeper of the checks and balances). We leave sticky notes around the house and in the cars, we write little "I love you" notes on windows and mirrors, even send cards through the mail or hide them in various places where they will be found weeks… or months down the road.

We run a ministry together. David does the heavy lifting outside the home—long hours, physical labor, leadership, and provision. I work from my home office, where I manage the ministry operations, keep the books balanced, write curriculum, oversee correspondence, and keep our vision moving forward. At the same time, I cook three meals a day, do the laundry, clean the house, and create a home that functions as a place of order, peace, and most importantly a refuge.

Different roles. Same mission. Equal value. No confusion.

When we get through our day, we actually love to come home to snuggle on the couch – together.

And sometimes, we do it naked.

Truth is, that, according to the world, that behavior is simply not "normal."

A dear, sweet friend of mine posted a meme on Face Book a while back, the meme depicted a marriage relationship stating that "marriage was ugly," that each person simply "put up" with one another, resolving to "deal" with life together. My initial comment was brief:

"That is so sad."

To which she asked why I felt that way.

My response to her was delayed by prayer and became the thought process behind the beginning of this book. Memes like that, convey a deeply distorted view on the marriage that God intended. However, it does describe the typical American marriage. Jesus says that marriage is a direct reflection of His relationship with the church. Marriage is two people who have become one. They are bound by Christ.

Marriage is not ugly. It is beautiful. I understood the meme – I just had an issue with the message that it way conveying:

> "You see the absolute worst in someone… they're so unlovable that they make you scream."

That is not how I chose to view my husband – ever. Nor how he will ever see me. We are not called to behave like that. We are not called to be "unlovable" we are called to love one another with kindness, gentleness and patience with all the self-control that it takes to ensure that we are not unlovable – even when they are.

Biblical marriage is one where we love each other through complete submission to one another – in and through Christ alone. That we love in a way that provides the other with a safe place to fall. That in and out of our homes we respect the other person without ever speaking harsh, rude, comments that would cause them hurt, embarrassment or shame – even unintended sarcasm.

I personally know that this is obtainable because I live it.

Years ago, however, I believed the connotations found in this meme:

> Marriage is ugly – it is two people fighting to stay together, disrespectful of the other person's feelings and allowing the non-Christian worldview to tell me that I had a "right," to announce my husband's flaws to the world.

But the biblical worldview is much different.

The Bible helps us by instructing us to focus on "that what is pure, holy and just" (Philippians 4:8, English Standard Version).[1]

Where there is any sign of discord, we are to communicate to one another lovingly and extract information from discussions that promote and provide understanding - not ammunition.

I suffered ugly marriages because I believed that was the way two people were destined to be.

Forty years ago, I walked away from David because of this very thing. I left a man after God's own heart who never spoke a mean, belittling word to me or about me – But rather when harsh words were spoken (usually by me) with demanding insults, it made him sad – not because I hurt him, but because he believed that I was hurting.

I believed that he was too good to be true, that he was somehow weak and refused to "fight back" I walked away. Had I married David back then, I would have shredded him.

You don't know me but, in the family, I grew up in, harsh words spoken in "jest" was a way of life. But they are harmful they destroy emotional safety, they lead to criticism and hurt feelings, betrayal and mistrust – they focus on all that is wrong, not what is right. And God says they are not allowed in His design for marriage.

Neither are ungodly expectations. Our expectations of one another are built on what Christ says about Himself, ourselves, and others. Expectations begin and end in the Bible, not in the home and have no place in marriage.

---

[1] *All Scripture is from the English Standard Version unless otherwise noted.*

And if we date "ugly" acting people, we will marry ugly acting people. Also, truth to ponder: If we act ugly, we attract ugly. Therefore, we need to set the standard for the women in our lives, especially our very own daughters. We have a responsibility to teach them to set the bar high – as High as Jesus' love for us and not settle for anything less – or allow them to become anything less.

For decades now, we have set the bar too low for people contemplating marriage. With this worldly depiction of marriage, it gives the illusion that there are no standards... that we must lower the bar and settle. We must either become one of those people who are disrespectful in their words, tone and body language – or we allow them to be in our circle of friends and family.

We cannot allow for sarcasm and expectations to take the place of encouragement, building up, and freedom to be all that God has created us to be.

The Bible gives us explicit guidelines whereby we are to realize that He is the standard to which we should strive to become and the standard by which we live – and that includes how we treat our spouse.

There is no Biblical love that includes complaining or gossiping about your spouse, there is no Biblical love that allows for harsh words, thoughts or attitudes that would cause harm, even in jest.

I did not know that could exist, but with Christ, all things are possible (Matt. 19:26). Godly marriages are built on Christ and they include respect, trust, kindness, gentleness and a whole lot of self-control – provided by the Spirit.

*For this reason I bow my knees before the Father, from whom every family in heaven and on earth is named, that according to the riches of his glory he may grant you to be strengthened with power through his Spirit in your inner being, so that Christ may dwell in your hearts through faith—that you, being rooted and grounded in love, may have strength to comprehend with all the saints what is the breadth and length and height and depth, and to know the love of Christ that surpasses knowledge, that you may be filled with all the fullness of God (Eph. 3:14-19).*

Now, with all of that being said, what I am not saying is that there will never be an issue or disagreement... Let's face it, two sinners are not always going to agree with one another... as a matter of fact, there will be an eyebrow (and elevated temperatures) raised – however, when those situations arise they are to be handled in loving conversation whereby a mutual respect for one another is realized and that understanding is the goal – not claiming rights or demands, let alone acting out in anger.

I personally do not know why, after 25 years of being mean, hurtful and using words, sex, and past pain as weapons, God would turn the tide of time and bring David back into my life; allowing me a life with a man who provides safety and security in and out of our home – I certainly don't deserve such a man, but He did it anyway.

But I do know this. I prayed that one day, I was going to be the woman God created me to be. That I would not be confrontational, but communicative. That I would not focus on bad habits or create chaos and that I would love with complete surrender and obedience and I would never again enter into a relationship whereby I was not honored, adored and respected... and I also knew by Scripture, that to have that, I had to be honorable, adorable, and respectful.

I know I have failed many times in this endeavor – but somehow – by some miraculous Spirit-shade of grace – my beloved sees me for the woman I intend to be – rather than the one that seeps out through the cracks.

It is my prayer that every woman sees marriage as the beautiful miracle that it is: A moment-by-moment divine intervention of the Holy Spirit working in and through two sinners who are bound by Him. Where their thoughts and words are under control and do no harm. Where they are led by the Spirit and are free to openly be all that God created them to be, knowing that they have someone in their corner praying for them and who respects the role that God has placed them in.

*"Set me as a seal upon your heart, as a seal upon your arm; for love is as strong as death, jealousy as cruel as the grave; its flames are flames of fire, a most vehement flame."*

*(Song of Solomon 8:6)*

# Introduction

It was one of those days... No... It had been one of those seasons! Chalk full of multiple projects that had all reached the deadline and needed to be completed and it was down to the wire time. Our ministry was off to a great beginning which required conferences, webpage building and social media interactions not to mention phone calls to make, conferences to attend, and press-releases to send.

In the midst of all the chaos, there was school – David finishing up his Master of Divinity and I was completing my undergrad degree. Amid my assignments there was the massive project for my husband's MDiv. that required my research and formatting skills, so he could put the project together and write the paper – all while he worked our business for 15 hours every day. And then there were the polishing touches for my ministry's training manual, teaching curriculum and student workbook, that had to be submitted prior to us speaking at a world-wide conference just a few months out. In-between were the phone calls from my adult daughter that required no less than 60 minutes of mommy time and involved lengthy discussions on parenting, marriage, recipes, finance 101, and career coaching.

I looked down at myself and realized I was still wearing my pink furry robe, purple fuzzy slippers and my hair had been tossed onto the top of my head, secured with a paper clip. The dog... a 150-pound Great Dane, that had slipped in unnoticed some time ago was now, lying next to me in my home office and she was covered from head to toe...

In something...

"What is that?" as I glanced at the trail of muck that led from the dog lying at my feet, down the hallway, and all the way to the back door...

"Really!" I said to my snoring dog, "I just vacuumed...

Or was that yesterday?" I wondered...

"Oh, I don't have time for this!" I thought, feeling the overwhelming urge to scream... but I knew the time was getting close for David to leave work and head home and I hadn't even thought about dinner – let alone pulling out the vacuum that I just knew had to be cleaned out before it could be used...

Ugh! I made my way to the kitchen and looked at the clock. Holy cow! I only had 35 minutes before he was to arrive home which meant five minutes before I got his "I'm coming home" phone call and I had no idea what I was cooking for dinner!! – Yet another task that would require more time than I had... especially since it would have to begin with cleaning the kitchen before I could even think about starting to cook.

"I wonder if the dishes in the dishwasher are clean or dirty?" I silently whispered to myself...

"Ugh!" I sighed, making my way to the hamburger laying in the sink that I had taken out freezer an hour earlier... Okay, maybe three---four hours... earlier...?

"How long can it stay there and still be good?" I thought, gazing at the reddish-brown lump of meat... "heavy sigh."

Sable, the dirty-filthy dog, had made her way out of the office into the family room and was reclining on our white leather sofa, all tucked up nice and comfy with the throw pillows under her dusty paws and dirt covered legs...

"Really?" I thought.

Vacuuming could take precious minutes that I simply did not have and to take something else out of the freezer would take too long! So, as I began contemplating my options, I realized that I could not greet my husband like this... Yet again...

I had to change clothes and do something with my hair before he walked through the door – So a quick shower had to be at the top of the list.

I continued through the family room into the bedroom, glancing over at the unmade bed piled high with the unfolded laundry and felt the overwhelming sense of frustration begin to well up inside me... "Something. Has. Got. To. Give!" I muttered.

No dinner, unmade bed, piles of laundry, dirty house, messy floors, disaster of a kitchen and an un-kept, unnerved, wiped out wife- "Wow!" I thought, what a sight to come home to.

Glancing over at the unmade bed once more, I realized how exhausted I was and a fleeting thought of "just one minute," raced through my mind.... But I quickly realized that being horizontal at that moment would lead to hours and that simply would not solve my issues, and I was running out of time! Knowing that my tired, hungry (and more than likely feeling a little neglected) husband was due to call at the precise time I would be in mid-lather, I sent him a text:

"Don't know what's for dinner.... So, when you arrive home, I'll be barefoot, naked, and in the kitchen."

Problem solved. ☺

*He had planned it all out – He wanted her to be just exactly right – so he stopped everything and carefully designed her.*

*Beyond the chemical compositions, the personal DNA:  She was to be beautiful – He took His time and formed her. He counted the hair on her head, her fingers and toes.  Then He chose the color of her eyes. He gave her a personality with humor and designed the way her mouth would move as she laughed. He gave her a voice that he would learn to recognize as her heart and a body that he would always desire.*

*Then He chose a color for her skin and placed little freckles here and there to give her character and then chose a color for her hair. He declared her excellent and her worth far more precious than jewels. He gave her heart purpose that her husband could always trust. He designed her specifically to do her husband good and not harm all of her days.*

*He designed her to be strong and to work willingly and hard. He gave her a sound mind and a nurturing spirit. He gave her courage to pursue dreams and to make sure that her family would pursue theirs. He gave her a spirit of love, grace and mercy. Designed purposefully and lovingly with courage and dignity. Man's perfect helper.*

*Then He presented her, as a finely crafted gift, not out of the dirt of the ground, but of the very flesh of humanity– the only creation ever presented by the direct hand of God to man.*

*Yes, she was fearfully and wonderfully made. She is woman. She "completes" the man. She is his glory and crown. And together they will become one flesh.*

*He who finds a wife finds a good thing (Pr. 18:22a).*

# The Cinderella Illusion

## Because Glass Slippers do not fit Real Life

*Surprise! That pumpkin was your carriage. The dog ate your slipper. What Prince? You mean the frog in the bathroom?*

Somewhere in our little girl dreams, we fantasize about going down the aisle, out the door to board our beautiful carriage that will take us down the golden road through the through the "happily-ever-after" forest that is just past the babbling brook leading us to our castle on the hill.

But then reality comes shining through the spotty, smeared window that we just spent an hour cleaning, and we realize that life just simply is not going to work that way.

Sometime after we get married, and the "honeymoon" is over we realize that it is not at all what the romance novels, fairy tales and love stories have told us it would be. Between the dirty dishes and dirty diapers, the hot flashes and grandbabies we lose ourselves and forget why we are here. All of a sudden, we wake up and wonder what are we even waking up for? It is just another day we will be overworked, underappreciated, and frankly, each day could easily be done in our sleep.

It is usually within that first-to-five-year mark when we are at about age 25 to 30, we discover those habits he has are not as cute as they once seemed to be, and he does not give us the attention we believe we deserve. He actually agrees with the fact that dinner "was missing a little something," and we think it's time for a change… someone who will need us more and appreciates our efforts – so we get pregnant. After our children are born and our quiet little world turns upside down, we come to the realization of having to learn how to power-sleep in between the feedings, the colic, diaper changes, teething, and tears – both theirs and ours.

About the five to ten-year mark or about age 30-40: Our kid's schedule demands more time than is humanly possible. We spend our time as taxi driver, short order cook/pizza delivery woman, and things within us start to change and we cannot for the life of us figure out what is happening to us except we are simply exhausted.

All the time.

After all this is the new millennium! Where women work – I mean really work not only do we feed the kids and do the laundry, sweep and mop the floors and get down on our knees to scrub the toilets - We get to hold down a job outside the home. And that is not including the new millennium schedule for our children! All while maintaining the "picture perfect" Proverbs 31 image of a godly woman.

Frankly that dreaded "women's movement" of the sixties now has us pulling double duty and, in some cases, triple duty! So now, in addition to our work inside the home, we get to clean up the messes of others outside the home.

How stupid are we?

Today's women work all day so we can get off in time to run to the grocery store and do the shopping, so we can get home to cook dinner, make the lunches for the next day before we sit down to eat for five minutes so that we can clean the dishes to get the kids ready for bed but not before helping them with homework, attending their recital, ball game or chess tournament. And remember – you are not just the chief cook and bottle washer – you are also the head cheerleader, encourager, support system, and healer of all boo-boos… Then we go to bed.

 At some point, we realize how long it has been since we have had a moment with our husbands, some much needed intimacy, let alone sex. So, we make a date, hire a sitter and set our sights on some quality time.

But after a long day and a wonderful night together, the only thing on your mind inadvertently comes out of your mouth – right in the midst of the "heat of passion," is "did you make the coffee?" The night suddenly falls silent as you feel the words escape your mouth… The expression on your husband's face says it all and you know you just blew it. But he has to understand… Right? He knows your schedule…. After all, if it wasn't for you…

Oh, but it gets better… right?

Somewhere around the fifteen to twenty-year mark of your marriage or age 40 to 50, you look in the mirror you notice that your cheek bones have moved to your jaw line, you have lines around your mouth that take parenthesis to a whole new level, your eye lids seem to have disappeared between the creases of wrinkles and you have to put on your reader-glasses just to apply eyeliner.

There are grey hairs that were not there yesterday – and they are coming out of your nose. And where your eyebrows suddenly disappear to, no one really knows…. unless they have taken up refuge in the mole that no longer resembles the beautiful Marilyn Monroe look of years gone by.

The good news is that you dropped a pant size, the bad news is that it is because what once was your curvy rear-end has now morphed into the tops of your now very long legs.

Bedtime in and of itself is a war zone of hot flashes and night sweats. Your husband no longer seems to desire sex… Or maybe he is simply too afraid to inquire of the possibility.

> "You don't see it slipping away, but somewhere between wearing maternity underwear under a flannel night gown to bed

and receiving a salad spinner for Christmas, the romance fades…"[2]

Somewhere in the midst of all of this your children make the decision they just can do it better on their own leaving you to re-design the "empty" nest - only upon completion of you newly-designed adult "time-out" reading room, they return to your doorstep demanding to know what on earth you have done to "their" room.

Maybe you and your happy hubby have retired?

And now you both are at home…

together….

all day…

Leaving you to wonder…. "What do we do now?"

We decide to get busy; we start a ministry… a women's payer group we attend once a week – but on the other five days…. well, there just does not seem to be a need to change out of our jammies, brush our hair let alone wash our face… as a matter of fact, we avoid the mirror at all costs. At some point, we realize that we have become roommates to our husbands, residing in separate rooms, keeping separate friends, and doing different activities… without each other.  And even though we try to convince ourselves we are the picture of contentment… what we really have become is complacent.

---

[2] Erma Bombeck, A Marriage Made in Heaven… or Too Tired for an Affair? (New York: HarperCollins, 1993), 147.

*"The wisest of women builds her house, but folly with her own hands, tears it down" (Pr. 14:1).*

**A Hard Look into the eyes of Complacency**

Everything in our life was perfect. From the outside looking in and from the inside looking out... we were the perfect, God-fearing, well educated, loving couple who never had an argument. We worked hard, went to church, read our Bibles, prayed for one another, did our devotions, mentored others – yet, through our busyness, we forgot our first love – until one day, it seemed, it exploded our hearts.

Statistics had taken its toll on me. I worked hard to keep my perfect GPA in tack. As a 51-year-old woman who hadn't taken a math class since early college days – it was more difficult than anything I could have imagined... and it was only getting harder as the weeks progressed.

My husband David had seen an increase in his personal training business and the increased workload began to take its toll. He was getting worn. Coupled with his frustration for the lack of ministry-usefulness began to flood his soul, and I chalked it up to just another "season of life."

He had completed his Master of Divinity, after completing a Masters in Apologetics, a total of seven years of school and four master's degrees- and he was ready for full-time ministry. The plan was to sell our personal training business of 30 years and move across the country and fulfill our call.

The business plan was done, the 501c3 completed, the accountant hired, the attorney hired, even someone to begin the application process for grants was in the works... yet after two years of having my home completely packed up, living on the bare essentials.... there we sat.

My husband's church internship, where he had hoped to gain insights to the development and management of a men's discipleship training program turned into a subtle statement of, "we don't need your help, just your attendance is required." His mentorship of a young man was met with a divorce. David felt hopeless and useless – not to mention the pain of acquiring an $80,000 student loan debt that seemed absolutely worthless.

But I missed it.

David got used to coming home for his one-hour lunch break, to a hastily made sandwich on the counter, and a frantic wife constantly reminding him of how "underwater" she felt with this class... To which he gently responded with, "I can make a sandwich honey, just go back to work."

Then there was that moment...

My gentle giant looked so sad. He was so worn. So, he was very frustrated with his life and his feelings of a lack of purpose. I reminded him that God was all over this, that it was just for a little while... And then I did the unthinkable...

In a rush to get back to my work, I said, "you're not frustrated or sad about us, are you?"

He began to tear up... then he took me into his arms to reassure me that it wasn't me... it was him.

Then, I simply turned around and headed straight back to my office.

Somehow, I didn't feel better. I knew what I had done and upon returning to my office cave, I hung my head and cried...

Another day passed, and he came home to me with tears in his eyes, as I handed him another sandwich and kiss on the cheek as I was about to rush back to the Greek formulas I was memorizing, and his question stopped me in my tracks.

He asked me, "Am I still a priority?"

At that moment, there was no escape. It was like someone had taken a sledgehammer to my heart.

He reacted to the look on my face, probably not knowing if I was going to turn the tables to blame him... and said, "forget that, I'm sorry, I know you're busy... it's just me."

"Of course, you are!" I protested. And with a hurried hug, and peck on the cheek, I went back to my office, with my wrecked heart and cried.

"What am I doing?" I thought. "What more can I possibly do!"

There was a game we used to play at school. Someone held a glass at one end of the school yard and we lined up in groups of two or more and ran across the school yard with our little spoons of water, trying desperately to fill the glass on the other end... but, because of our hurriedness, the water would spill out of our spoons and the glass took forever to fill.

My husband's cup was empty. He would stand, patiently, on the other side of our marriage as I ran past him with my little tablespoon of "encouraging words" but they were only partially meaningful by the time they got to him and his glass was left with just a trickle of nourishment.

The Bible tells us to "walk worthy of the calling to which you have been called" (Eph. 4:1) – As a married woman, I am called to be a wife. I have been entrusted with a gift from the Lord to care for until He returns. I am commanded to remember that we are one flesh and when he hurts, I hurt.

We are called to bring glory and honor to God in all we do – and I am called to walk worthy of that call by bringing honor and glory to God in my marriage. Through loving my husband, God is glorified. I am commanded to not just say the words, but to walk the walk, with all humility, patience, gentleness, bearing with him in love (Eph. 4:2), remembering that the goal is to "maintain the unity of the Spirit in the bond of peace" (Eph. 4:3).

I was not humble... I was boasting about my busyness.

I wasn't being patient... I was being frantic, and without speaking the words: I was reminding him of the importance of statistics in a research psychology degree – for the future of our ministry - and that he needed to just deal with it.

There is no "gentleness" when you ignore someone's pain – or gloss over it with a Scripture – especially when that chosen verse is twisted to inflict more pain or boost one's own agenda.

Unity is not: I'm doing statistics... you are working to provide... this is my lot – that is yours, there is nothing peaceful about being divided.

Ephesians 4 continues to remind us of God's commands, and it was during this season of discord, that I was reading that particular chapter. (Hmmm, imagine that).

The next morning a revelation occurred, as I was praying for my husband. I was asking how God would use me to calm his heart, so I could get back to this class that was overwhelming my mind...

I never realized that He would tell me to stop. Not quit. But just stop.

With much agonizing over the approaching deadline of two very lengthy assignments including one exam that required two chapters of reading – my first reaction was, "That's not even logical, Lord! Do you know how much money we have invested in our education? I have a responsibility to be a good steward of our money."

"Stop." Was His response. "Listen to me," is what I heard.

As I opened my Bible, He spoke:

No longer are you to be tossed to and fro by the waves of this world... Speak truth – but do it in love.

Grow UP!

You and your husband, that I gave you, are of one body, joined and held together, fully equipped – but they must be working properly to do good.

You must no longer "walk" as you once did – believing that an education is more important than giving your husband your attention- right now, he needs you and I have entrusted you to be there for him – you are his perfect helper (Gen. 2:18).

Help him.

Renew your mind, in the Spirit – put away your deceitful desires of pacifying him – and love him with your whole heart – with all righteousness and holiness.

Give no opportunity to the devil. Quit taking advantage of your husband's love for you – work your marriage and labor honestly – put your priorities in order.

Quit speaking to pacify and placate his feelings – they are valid to me; they must be valid to you – so speak words that build him up – give grace.

Do not grieve my Spirit with bitterness, wrath, anger, malice, clamor and slander – because you are not getting your way.

Right now – from this moment forward – remember your calling – and love your husband with all kindness – being tenderhearted and forgiving – just as Christ forgave you. (Eph. 4:17-32; Gen. 2:18, paraphrased)

Being called to godly womanhood is hard. But we cannot serve two masters – we will hate one and love the other (Matt. 6:24). I didn't realize that trying to "be responsible, dedicated, hardworking, and focused, student" was taking priority over my husband's needs – and my responsibility to fulfill those needs.

I didn't realize that the seven-night cruise that I purchased to help him relax, the new George-Jetson watch I bought him so he could get his text messages on his wrist, or the clean house and perfectly seasoned ribs I cooked, was not going to compensate for the face-to-face, uninterrupted attention from me, that he needed so desperately at this particular season in his life.

David needed to know that although he wasn't being used in his internship program, that his wife wanted him desperately. He needed to know that although he could not save the marriage of the man he was mentoring, that his marriage was solid. David needed a refuge to come home to – a place where he could find refreshment and renewal from his busy 15-hour days.

*Whoever brings blessing will be enriched, and one who waters will himself be watered (Pr. 11:25).*

My gifts, trips, hastily spoken words, kisses on the cheek, or quick hugs were not enough. He needed to know... see... feel... he needed to believe... that I was passionately and desperately in love with him. That I respected who he was as a man and the leader of our home, and as the love – and lover - of my life

*Let your fountain be blessed, and rejoice in the wife of your youth, a lovely deer, a graceful doe. Let her breasts fill you at all times with delight; be intoxicated always in her love (Pr. 5:18-19).*

That same passion that I was pouring into statistics – needed to be interrupted and redirected onto and into my husband's heart – and that meant I needed to stop, reorganize, and prioritize. I needed to be more focused on Biblical womanhood, than Super-womanhood.

**Priority #1 – Prayer for my man:**

I began to be more focused on prayers for my husband, prayers that were wrapped in Scripture and that were specific to his needs, wants, and desires. Prayers that would make a direct impact into his soul and his particular "season of life."

**Priority #2 – Greet him face to face.**

When he walked through the door, I set a timer as to stop working so that I was there to meet him at the door – take his gear, open the door, whatever I needed to do to let him know that he was a welcome sight to my heart.

**Priority #3 – Making words count.**

I made sure that when he spoke, I stopped what I was doing, put my phone down, turned down my show on television, closed my computer, to look him in those sweet baby-blue eyes. I chose to make my heart listen – for clarity and understanding of his heart. I held every one of my busy little thoughts captive – praying before I spoke, making sure I was building up, not tearing down, and praying that I wasn't talking more than I had to. I prayed that the words I spoke were meaningful, that they would build him up and be what he needed to hear, not just what I wanted to say.

**Priority #4 – Make a direct impact.**

I focused my kisses to be ones that would not be forgotten – but to be gently, intentionally placed on those sweet lips I held between my hands and that they were delivered with deliberate passion.

**Priority #5 – Romans 12:2 – Let God change the way you think.**

I made a choice to set aside my thoughts of what I felt I needed to get done, and trusted that God would take care of it – even if it meant supernaturally opening my mind to realize Greek equations in a way I never thought I could – and if it meant the house didn't get vacuumed or I was making reservations instead of dinner - so be it. I trusted that

Biblical womanhood was where God wanted me to be and if I put my priorities in place and walked in a manner worthy of my calling as a Biblical woman, then everything else would fall in place.

That's God's design and it works every time.

*"I relieved your shoulder of the burden; your hands were freed from the basket. In distress you called, and I delivered you (Ps. 81:6-7b).*

# ✦ DEVOTIONAL — THE CINDERELLA ILLUSION ✦

## Because Glass Slippers do not fit Real Life

*A Note Before You Begin*

*These devotionals aren't drive-through prayers. They're meant to take time—real time. So slow down. The next chapter isn't going anywhere. Sit with the Word. Let it expose what needs exposing. Then deal with it.*

*Here's the ground rule—and it's not optional:*

*Every prayer in this book begins with repentance. Why? Because Scripture is clear: unconfessed sin clouds discernment, fractures intimacy, and absolutely hinders our prayers. God isn't impressed by polished words attached to an unrepentant heart.*

*So we start here. Every time:*

**Before I ask You to _______, I confess where I have _______.**

*No skipping ahead. No spiritual gymnastics. No pretending.*

*This isn't my idea—it's God's pattern:*

- *Daniel 9*
- *Nehemiah 1*
- *Psalm 51*
- *Isaiah 6*

*If you want God to move, start by getting honest.*

Ouch!

*"Blows that wound cleanse away evil. Strokes make clean the innermost parts" (Pr. 20:30).*

## REFOCUS: Doctrine/Truth

*"Whatever is true, whatever is honorable, whatever is just, whatever is pure, whatever is lovely... think about these things." Philippians 4:8*

That same passion I was pouring into statistics needed to be interrupted and redirected into my husband's heart. It meant stopping, reorganizing, and prioritizing. It meant being more focused on biblical womanhood than on super-womanhood.

## REPRIORITIZE: Action/Obedience

- **Priority #1 – Pray for Your Man**

  Pray for your husband with Scripture, specific to his needs and season of life.

  *"The prayer of a righteous person has great power as it is working." James 5:16*

- **Priority #2 – Greet Him Face to Face**

  Be present. Stop what you're doing when he arrives and welcome him home.

  *"Her husband is known in the gates when he sits among the elders of the land" (Pr. 31:23).*

- **Priority #3 – Make Words Count**

  Choose words that build, not break. Listen before speaking.

  "A gentle tongue is a tree of life, but perverseness in it breaks the spirit." Proverbs 15:4


- **Priority #4 – Make a Direct Impact**

  Let your affection communicate love and belonging.

  *"Let him kiss me with the kisses of his mouth! For your love is better than wine" ( Song 1:2).*


- **Priority #5 – Let God Change the Way You Think**

  Trust God more than your to-do list.

  *"Do not be conformed to this world but be transformed by the renewal of your mind…" (Rom 12:2).*

**THE BOTTOM LINE:**

When we reorder our priorities according to God's design, peace enters our homes. Our husbands feel cherished, our hearts find rest, and our marriages begin to breathe again.

**REFLECT: Journal Prompts**

1. What specific way can I serve my husband this week?
2. Which area of my attitude or words need more grace?
3. How can I make our home a stronger refuge of peace?

**RESPOND: Prayer**

*Father, before I ask You to move, I confess where I have resisted Your will in __________.*

*Lord, renew my mind and reorder my heart. Teach me to love with patience, speak with gentleness, and welcome my husband the way You welcome me. Amen.*

# Still His Bride

## When Grace Outshines Gravity

Today I turned sixty. Yes, today, December 15, 2025.

They say age is just a number—and today, as I turn 60, I can confidently say it has *done* a number on me.

The number of chins now living under the original.

The number of new age spots auditioning for lead roles on my face.

The number of noises my body makes when I stand up that should come with a warning label.

But here's the thing— 60 also comes with a number of gifts.

The number of battles I survived.

The number of lessons I learned the hard way so I don't have to repeat them.

The number of opinions I no longer feel obligated to explain, defend, or soften.

I've earned every line, every laugh mark, every scar, and every story.

Sixty isn't the beginning of the end— it is the age where wisdom finally outranks insecurity. Where peace beats pretension, and joy doesn't need anyone's permission.

So, here's to 60! Seasoned, sanctified, still standing, and still laughing.

Because if age is just a number, this one tells a *very* good story.

*"Charm is deceitful, and beauty is vain, but a woman who fears the Lord is to be praised" (Pr. 31:30).*

Somewhere between gravity doing its thing and grace doing *its* thing, something surprising happens.

I realize I'm still his bride.

Not *used to be* – when my metabolism was a team player.

Not *once upon a time.*

Still.

**The Lie We Start Believing Too Early**

Long before the wrinkles show up, women are quietly discipled by lies:

That desirability has an expiration date.

That romance is for the young.

That passion fades because it's supposed to.

That after a certain age, you should be grateful—but not expectant.

The world tells women that aging is something to fight, hide, apologize for, or joke about until we believe the punchline.

And too many Christian women absorb these lies, dressed up as "humility."

"I'm not attractive anymore."

"I don't feel sexy."

"I've let myself go."

"He can't possibly still desire me."

But our husbands think, "She is beautiful. Why is she changing her clothes in the closet?" *(True story, not me, but a woman who changed her clothes in the closet from the time they got married and all throughout their 55+ year marriage!).*

But Scripture never speaks of a woman losing her worth with age.

It speaks of her *gaining glory.*

> *"Gray hair is a crown of glory; it is gained in a righteous life"* (Pr. 16:31).

Grace does not compete with gravity.

Grace outshines it.

**Still Desired, Still Chosen**

Here are some things that we don't say out loud often enough:

Your husband did not marry a body.

He married *you.*

The woman who has walked through life with him.

The woman who has carried joy and sorrow, laughter and loss.

The woman who knows his rhythms, his weaknesses, his silence, and his soul.

And if your husband is a godly man, his attraction has matured along with his love.

Men don't age like women—but godly men *deepen*.

What once caught their eye now holds their heart.

And our men are not conducting a forensic audit on our thighs. They're just happy you're in the room and if you just happen to be without clothing… Bonus!

Scripture gives us permission— no, *confirmation*— to believe this:

> *"Many women have done excellently, but you surpass them all"* (Pr. 31:29).

That verse wasn't written to a twenty-year-old. It was written to a woman who has lived long enough to know better – and love deeper.

**The Mirror Is Not the Measure**

At some point, most women begin negotiating with the mirror (especially the magnified mirror):

Lighting is adjusted.

Angles are negotiated.

Clothes become camouflage.

We don't just notice change— we interpret it.

And often, we interpret it harshly.

But the mirror was never meant to be the *authority*.

The **Word** was.

God does not describe His bride as fading.

He describes her as being made ready.

> *"Christ loved the church and gave Himself up for her… so that He might present the church to Himself in splendor"* (Eph. 5:25–27).

Marriage is the lived-out parable of that truth.

You are not becoming less lovely.

You are becoming more *established* – The biblical way of saying: solid, secure, and no longer impressed by nonsense!

**From Insecure to Anchored**

There is a quiet confidence that comes with age— not because everything is perfect, but because fewer things get to *rule* you.

You've survived disappointment.

You've endured seasons you never thought you would.

You've learned that feelings are not facts and that faithfulness matters more than flash. And you also learned that wearing uncomfortable shoes is a lie from the pit of hell.

And here's the unexpected gift: When insecurity loosens its grip, intimacy deepens. Not the kind driven by performance or comparison— but the kind rooted in safety, trust, and love.

This is where many women miss the invitation.

They think aging disqualifies intimacy, when in reality, it *purifies* it (there is something incredibly attractive about a woman who is not auditioning anymore).

**Still His Bride—By Covenant, Not Cosmetics**

Marriage is not maintained by youth.

It is sustained by covenant.

*"I will betroth you to Me forever"* (Hosea 2:19).

And when a woman believes that—really believes it—she stops shrinking and starts inhabiting her life again.

She laughs more freely.

She moves with ease.

She shows up without apology.

She changes clothes with the doors open and lights on again.

Not because she's trying to compete with her younger self— but because she's no longer afraid of her present one.

So yes—gravity may have had its say…but grace has the victory. And I'm not hiding in the shadows of age— I'm still his bride, barefoot, naked, and very much at home.

Remember, he loves you and desires to be loved by you.

*"Your stature is like that of the palm, and your breasts like clusters of fruit. I said, "I will climb the palm tree; I will take hold of its fruit." May your breasts be like clusters of grapes on the vine, the fragrance of your breath like apples." (Song, 7:7-8).*

*When Grace Outshines Gravity*

**REFOCUS: Doctrine/Truth**

**Aging does not diminish your worth—it displays God's grace.**

In Christ, you are not growing less lovely but being made radiant by grace. Your beauty is not defined by youth but by covenantal love, rooted in the God who delights in His bride. Just as Christ presents His Church in splendor, so too marriage tells the story of enduring desire, sanctified intimacy, and steadfast love. Gravity may mark the body, but grace marks the soul—and in the eyes of your husband and your God, you are still the beloved bride.

*"He who began a good work in you will bring it to completion at the day of Jesus Christ" (Phil. 1:6).*

**REPRIORITIZE: Action/Obedience**

- **Reclaim God's Definition of Beauty**

  Stop allowing the mirror—or culture—to define what God has already declared good.

  *"Charm is deceitful, and beauty is vain, but a woman who fears the Lord is to be praised" (Pr. 31:30).*

Preach truth to your heart daily. Replace self-criticism with Scripture.

- **Live Present, Not Apologetic**

  Do not shrink back because of age, change, or season.

  *"Stand firm and let nothing move you" (1 Cor. 15:58).*

  Your presence matters—in your marriage, your home, and your calling.

- **Embrace Confidence Rooted in Covenant**

  Your identity is not tied to how you look, but to whom you belong.

  *"I am my beloved's, and my beloved is mine" (Song 6:3).*

  Confidence grounded in covenant brings peace to the home and security to the marriage.

- **Cultivate Joy Without Permission**

  Joy is not earned by youth; it is cultivated by gratitude.

  *"The joy of the Lord is your strength" (Neh. 8:10).*

  Laugh. Delight. Be fully present in your life.

- **Remember Who Holds You**

  Gravity pulls—but grace sustains.

  *"Underneath are the everlasting arms" (Deut. 33:27).*

  You are upheld by a faithful God who does not abandon His work halfway through.

**THE BOTTOM LINE:**

A woman who understands grace does not fear aging. She knows her worth is not expiring — it is deepening. Her beauty is not diminishing — it is maturing. Her marriage is not fragile — it is covenantally secure.

She is still chosen.

Still cherished.

Still desired.

Still His bride.

And she stands—barefoot, naked, and unashamed—exactly where God has planted her.

**REFLECT: Journal Prompts**

1. Where have I believed cultural lies about aging instead of biblical truth?
2. How has God used time, experience, and hardship to deepen my wisdom?
3. In what ways have I begun to hide or shrink instead of living confidently?
4. What would change if I fully believed I am still desired and cherished?
5. Which Scripture from this chapter can I meditate on this week?

**RESPOND: Prayer**

*Before I ask You to heal what is broken, I confess where I have held onto offense, bitterness, or self-protection instead of trusting You.*

*Lord,*

*Thank You for every year You have given me. Thank You for the lessons, the growth, and the grace that has carried me this far. Help me to see myself through Your Word—not through fear, comparison, or culture. Teach me to walk confidently in my season, anchored in covenant and clothed in grace. Let my life reflect joy, wisdom, and trust in You— as a woman who knows she is still Your daughter and still her husband's bride. Amen.*

# Called to Duty

## Biblical Womanhood Lived Without Apology

*"The wisest of women builds her house, but folly with her own hands tears it down." (Pr. 14:1)*

Let's just go ahead and say it out loud:

Duty.

There. I said it.

You probably flinched a little. Maybe your eye twitched. Somewhere in the distance, a feminist podcast host just dropped her latte.

The word *duty* has become so unpopular that we treat it like an uninvited guest at girls' night. We tolerate it when absolutely necessary—tax season, jury summons, maybe flossing—but we certainly don't want it anywhere near marriage, femininity, or sex.

We prefer softer words now. Words like *journey*, *self-expression*, *authenticity*, or my personal favorite—*boundaries*.

But Scripture? Scripture didn't get the memo.

*"Let God be true though every one were a liar" (Rom. 3:4).*

The Bible speaks unapologetically about our responsibilities as Christians. This is our duty—not as oppression, but as privilege. Not as obligation chained to guilt, but as calling rooted in covenant.

We made a covenant with Christ when we surrendered our life to Him and publicly honored Him in baptism. That covenant is non-negotiable.

The same is true in our covenant to our husbands – and our responsibilities (duties) that are intermingled with that covenant.

And here's the uncomfortable truth we don't like to admit: Every meaningful relationship in your life already operates on duty.

You have a duty to your children.

You have a duty to your employer.

You even have a duty to stop at red lights, no matter how late you're running.

But the moment we apply that word to biblical womanhood or marriage, we recoil like someone just suggested eating kale on purpose.

Yet Scripture dares to tell us something radical:

A biblical woman's duties are not burdens—they are acts of worship.

And yes… that includes the kitchen and the bedroom.

Before you panic, clutch your pearls, or prepare an email explaining why this chapter "feels a little legalistic," let me assure you of this: Duty flows from grace, not pressure.

It is not about earning love.

It is about living faithfully in response to it.

**When in doubt, just ask.**

Let me set the stage: Our home in Scottsdale was tiny. But it did have a *gorgeous* soaking tub in the master bath. It was truly a delight—until you realized the room itself was so small, it made a tuna can feel spacious. Not to mention, it was ADA-compliant, which meant the layout was designed for accessibility, but that also meant if both the shower door and the bathroom door weren't opened in the exact right order, they would collide like two bumper cars at an amusement park.

Now, one day my daughter came to visit, and naturally, she was thrilled by the tub. "Can I use it?" she asked, and I, being the ever-loving mother of course, gave her the spa treatment her entitled little heart felt like it deserved.

As we walked into the bathroom, I noticed the towel was lying on the floor. It's something I'm used to—honestly, I didn't think much of it, so I bent down to pick it up. But then... my daughter, ever on the lookout for anything she can criticize about our marriage, went ballistic!

Who needs TV drama when you've got family?

"I cannot believe he wouldn't pick up his towel! Do you have to do everything for him?!"

This was a really big deal for her. Apparently, this towel situation had launched her into a full-on meltdown.

Now, here's the thing: I had never thought about the towel before. But that night when Dave came home—my 6'0", 250-pound, bodybuilder of a man— I told him about the incident. He immediately apologized – but proceeded to explain why he sometimes forgets:

To put the towel back on the towel rack, he has to first close the shower door, in order to open the door to the bedroom… he uses the towel to cover himself before getting dressed, which means that to put the towel back into the bathroom on the rack, he (again, six-foot tall, 5 foot wide), has to open the bathroom door, enter the bathroom, close the bathroom door to open the shower door… are you getting the picture?

So, yeah, occasionally, the towel ends up on the floor with the intention of getting it back to the rack – sometimes it made it there – and sometimes it did not.

Who cares?

Well, *she* did, that's for sure!

**The Case of the Laundry Basket (Exhibit B)**

In yet another "gotcha" moment, my daughter noticed something else about Dave.

Apparently, she had been conducting a full-scale domestic audit.

She pointed out that David often hangs his clothes *over* the laundry basket instead of placing them *inside* the basket.

Now mind you — this is the same daughter who, if left to her own devices, wouldn't recognize a laundry basket as her own possession if it waved at her and asked for mercy. But I digress.

"So… why don't his clothes ever make it *into* the basket?" she asked, eyebrows raised, case already built.

I shrugged. "So what?"

But since the towel incident had already made it to trial, we decided to consult the accused.

When David came home, we asked him why his clothes were draped over the basket instead of tossed inside like the rest of civilized humanity.

Without missing a beat, he explained — calmly, thoughtfully — that he, as a personal fitness trainer, sweats at work and doesn't want to throw damp, sweaty clothes into the basket where they could soil or mildew my nice clothing. Instead, he hangs them over the edge to dry until laundry day.

And just like that, Exhibit B collapsed.

What had looked like sloppiness was actually consideration.

What had been framed as incompetence was, in reality, courtesy.

And what was assumed to be a flaw turned out to be forethought.

It's amazing how often a simple explanation dismantles a well-rehearsed accusation.

**From Towels to Theology**

And here's the thing…

Neither the towel nor the laundry basket was the real issue.

The real issue was *interpretation.*

Both situations were perfect examples of how quickly small, ordinary behaviors can be misread, judged, and assigned, meaning that they were never meant to carry. A towel becomes evidence of laziness. A laundry basket becomes proof of incompetence. And suddenly, a good man is standing trial over household logistics.

This is how marriages get wounded—not by sin, but by assumptions.

And if we're honest, women are particularly skilled at this. We notice details. We connect dots. We tell stories in our heads. Sometimes those stories are true. And sometimes… they're fiction wrapped in confidence.

What saved these moments in our home was not correction or confrontation— it was understanding. We asked. We listened. And when we did, the narrative changed.

Which brings us to our duty as biblical wives.

Scripture does not call us to be our husband's public prosecutor, character analyst, or moral referee. It calls us to be his helper, his protector, and his greatest advocate. Our duty is not to magnify his imperfections, but to interpret him with charity, to assume the best, and to guard his dignity— <u>especially</u> in the presence of others.

*"Finally, brothers, whatever is true, whatever is honorable, whatever is just, whatever is pure, whatever is lovely, whatever is commendable, if there is any excellence, if there is anything worthy of praise, think about these things" (Phil. 4:8).*

This is not weakness.

This is wisdom.

Biblical duty flows from covenant love, not cultural suspicion. It means we do not allow outside voices—well-meaning or otherwise—to redefine our husbands through a lens of criticism. Instead, we filter every observation through grace, respect, and honor.

A biblical wife understands that her first responsibility is not to analyze her husband, but to stand with him. Not to correct him publicly, but to cover him faithfully. Not to collect evidence, but to cultivate unity.

This is where duty begins.

Not with perfection.

Not with control.

But with a heart committed to love, honor, and covenant faithfulness—rooted in the gospel and lived out in the ordinary rhythms of everyday life.

> *"Steadfast love and faithfulness preserve the king and his throne is established forever" (Pr. 20:28).*

Let your husband know that he is still the king of his castle.

I realize that people, especially us women, do not like that word, "duty." But the reality is – we have duties. And those "duties" are, simply put, divinely appointed responsibilities that glorify God, serve others, and sanctify the believer in everyday life. It also serves as an example to the outside world looking in.

Duty flows from covenant grace, not cultural pressure. It's not about earning favor but living faithfully in light of the gospel. A biblical woman's duties are her daily acts of worship — ordinary obedience that makes the extraordinary love of Christ visible in every corner of her home.

Including your bedroom. In the context of this particular book - our wifely duties are also designed and intended to keep our marriage out of the danger zone of complacency.

*You have captivated my heart, my sister, my bride; you have captivated my heart with one glance of your eyes, with one jewel of your necklace. How beautiful is your love, my sister, my bride! How much better is your love than wine, and the fragrance of your oils than any spice! (Song 4:9-10).*

If there is one thing in my many, many years of marriage, that I have learned is that I love being a woman. The sorry thing is that I did not learn that until I was in my late-forties. The way that I learned about my love for womanhood, was when I discovered what the Word of God had to say about women and the more I read, the more I began to understand that we are a true delight and the apple of God's eye.

We, women, unlike our male counterparts are delightfully different – equal in humanity, yet different in our role and responsibilities.

**Duties of a Biblical Woman**

**Duty to Worship**

*"You shall love the Lord your God with all your heart and with all your soul and with all your might." (Deut 6:5).*

Worship is not confined to Sunday mornings. A Biblical woman's first duty is daily, wholehearted worship — offering every moment, every task, every thought to the glory of God (1 Cor. 10:31).

**Practical Expression:** Morning prayer, Scripture reading, singing hymns & dancing to Christian songs while cooking, and practicing gratitude in the mundane.

---

**Duty to the Word**

*"Man shall not live by bread alone, but by every word that comes from the mouth of God" (Matt. 4:4).*

A Biblical woman anchors her emotions, decisions, and priorities in the sufficiency of Scripture. She studies not for self-help, but for sanctification. To learn who God is so that she knows what God expects of her.

**Practical Expression:** Daily Bible reading, catechism memorization, journaling through Scripture, teaching her children biblical truth.

---

**Duty to Prayer and Intercession**

*"Pray without ceasing" (1 Thes. 5:17).*

Prayer is both a privilege and a responsibility. She intercedes for her husband, her children, community, family, friends, her church, and her own sanctification — trusting that God moves through prayer.

**Practical Expression:** Covering her husband's work, trials, and temptations in prayer, praying over her children's hearts (whether they are at home or away), praying for the church's leaders, the community, as well as state and national authorities.

**Duty to Her Home**

*"The wisest of women builds her house, but folly with her own hands tears it down" (Pr 14:1).*

The home is a covenant space — a microcosm of the Kingdom. Managing it well is not mere domestic work; it's sacred stewardship.

**Practical Expression:** Creating an atmosphere of peace, hospitality, and order that reflects God's beauty and truth. Creating a refuge, a safe place to fall.

---

**Duty to Her Children (or Spiritual Children)**

*"These words that I command you today shall be on your heart. You shall teach them diligently to your children" (Deut. 6:6–7).*

She disciples the next generation — whether her biological children or those entrusted to her spiritual influence — grounding them in truth and grace.

**Practical Expression:** Reading Scripture together, modeling repentance, showing mercy, and teaching biblical discernment and self-control.

**Duty to Serve the Body of Christ**

*"As each has received a gift, use it to serve one another, as good stewards of God's varied grace" (1 Pt 4:10).*

The Biblical woman recognizes her gifts as tools for the edification of the church. Her service isn't for attention — it's worship in action.

**Practical Expression:** Teaching the younger women, hosting Bible studies, serving in ministries, mentoring new female believers either in person or on a podcast, writing a book or a blog, and/or using social media as the town square.

Warning: you may lose friends and not get invited to many gatherings – and prepare to be persecuted, ridiculed, and mocked – like a lot!

---

**Duty to Steward Herself**

*"Do you not know that your body is a temple of the Holy Spirit within you...?" (1 Cor. 6:19).*

She honors God through self-discipline — stewarding her time, body, and emotions as gifts entrusted to her for His glory.

Another unpopular statement: Being late is flat-out disrespectful to your husband. We know how long it's going to take us to get ready to go somewhere, so please, allow for extra time or at least inform your husband that you will need "X amount of time" to get ready and that way he can prepare for what comes next. It also teaches your children (if they are still at home) another form of how to honor their parents – also sets a standard they can live up to – and teach others.

**Practical Expression:** Time management, healthy rest, exercise, modesty, self-control, mental renewal, and treating herself as one redeemed and dearly loved.

## Duty to Speak Life

*"She opens her mouth with wisdom, and the teaching of kindness is on her tongue" (Pr. 31:26).*

Every word a woman speaks either builds or breaks. Her duty is to speak truth seasoned with grace.

**Practical Expression:** Choosing gentleness over sarcasm, encouragement over criticism, truth over flattery.

## Duty to Reflect Christ in All Things

*"For we are His workmanship, created in Christ Jesus for good works, which God prepared beforehand" (Eph. 2:10).*

Her ultimate duty — and delight — is to mirror Christ in her home, her marriage, her motherhood, and her ministry.

**Practical Expression:** Living intentionally, repenting quickly, forgiving freely, and loving sacrificially.

## Duty to Her Husband

*"Wives, submit to your own husbands, as to the Lord." — Ephesians 5:22*

Submission, in Biblical theology, is not subservience but sanctified service. It's the joy of reflecting the Church's love for Christ. Her husband is her first and foremost ministry. Her marriage is the reflection of that covenant. It's the joy of emulating the Church's love for Christ. Her duty is to respect, honor, encourage, and support <u>her husband's</u> leadership as unto the Lord.

*Side Note: Contrary to the popular belief here in the Bible-belt.. This command of being obedient, submissive, or subject to is limited to "her own husband." In 1 Peter3:1, Peter is intentional with his language: "wives, be subject to **your own husbands**," holding up Sarah as an example who obeyed Abraham within the bounds of her covenant, **<u>not</u>** as a universal submission to all male authority (1 Peter 3:5–6).*

*The assumption that all women owe obedience to all men is not Christianity; it is cultural patriarchy wearing church clothes. Scripture does not grant men blanket authority over women by virtue of gender, geography, or church membership. That is a hard no. Authority in marriage is covenantal, not communal. A woman is not under the leadership of "the men," the deacons, the elders' opinions, or the self-appointed male voices of Christian culture. She is under Christ, and then—by God's design—under **her own husband**. Anything beyond that is an overreach Scripture does not authorize.*

**Practical Expression:** Speaking words that build rather than belittle or embarrass (whether at home, in public, or in his absence), greeting him with joy, being trustworthy and faithful (Pr. 31:11–12).

Let me make one more point—because this matters.

Women who refuse to take their husband's last name are dishonoring their covenant. And no, hyphenating it doesn't fix the issue—it just softens the rebellion.

When I've asked women why they won't take their husband's name, or to be called "Ms." Rather than "Mrs."… and the answers usually sound noble:

*"I'm honoring my parents."*

*"I don't want to lose my identity."*

Let's tell the truth.

Your parents are not your covenant.

Your identity is not your surname.

And fear is not a biblical justification.

Scripture is clear:

*"Therefore a man shall leave his father and his mother and hold fast to his wife, and they shall become one flesh" (Genesis 2:24).*

Leave.

Cleave.

One.

Not partially.

Not symbolically.

Not with a foot still planted in your daddy's house.

When you marry, your husband becomes your headship. You are no longer operating under your father's authority—you are entering a new covenantal covering. To cling to your former name as a badge of independence is to misunderstand what marriage actually is.

Leave and cleave. One flesh. One name. A public declaration of your vows.

In Biblical theology, duty flows from covenant grace, not cultural pressure. It's not about earning favor but living faithfully in light of the gospel. Her duties (responsibilities) are her daily acts of worship — ordinary obedience that makes the extraordinary love of Christ visible in every corner of her home.

*"Likewise, wives, be subject to your own husbands, so that even if some do not obey the word, they may be won without a word by the conduct of their wives, when they see your respectful and pure conduct"* (1Peter 3:1-2).

I have been a practicing Christian for many decades, but I honestly did not fully understand my duty as a Christian meant more than going through the motions of reading the Bible, going to church, and serving on a committee – or even marrying a Pastor. Rather, it meant being in a personal relationship with Christ.

It is only through an intimate relationship with Christ that we develop understanding of who God is and what it means to not only accept Him as Savior – but also to understand that He is Lord and therefore He has non-negotiable standards which are conveyed in His Word.

It was when I came to that realization, I began studying – not just reading – but really studying the Word, and discovered that there is a purpose to my life that goes beyond what I think is purposeful, and it is found in one very simple principal: "Whatever you do, do all to the glory of God" (1 Cor. 10:31b).

I had to take a good hard look at how I was glorifying the Lord in my marriage - my whole marriage - including in the bedroom. Women tend to buy in to the attitudes of the world that magnifies sex as a weapon used to get men and hold them in submission to our whims - but that is far from God's intention for sex. And sex is not only to be used as a "multiplier" either. Sex and the orgasms that go along with them are good - they are very good... one might say, "fruitful."

One of the issues I had for a while was holding my husband hostage to some trauma I had experienced. He did not do it. So, why was I holding him responsible for the sin of another?

We must repent if we are indeed doing this, and we must pray for a renewed commitment to the covenant we have made to our husbands to ensure that all of our duties as a biblical wife, including our sexual duties to our husband are fulfilling (not just being fulfilled).

This is the grateful response of a redeemed heart that has been captivated by grace. Each time we are intimate with our spouse, it is an act of obedience - and worship - not something that is done out of compulsion

- there is no "fake it till you make it." It is done out of covenant love: First for Christ, and then for the husband He has entrusted to your care.

**A Home is Never Neutral.**

It is either being built up— or quietly dismantled.

*"I passed by the field of a sluggard, by the vineyards of a [wo]man lacking sense. Behold it was overgrown with thorns, the ground covered with nettles and its stone wall broken down..." (Pr. 24:30-31).*

Scripture does not reduce a woman's role in the home to chores or checklists. It frames her work as *construction*. Every word spoken, every assumption made, every tone chosen, every reaction restrained or released is laying brick or swinging a wrecking ball.

The home is a covenant space—a living, breathing microcosm of the Kingdom of God. What happens inside its walls tells the truth about what we believe outside of them. It is where theology becomes tangible, where grace either settles in or is driven out.

Managing a home well is not mere domestic labor. It is sacred stewardship.

A biblical wife understands that her duty is not to run a household like a tribunal, but to cultivate it as a refuge—a place where her husband can land safely when the world has worn him down. A place where mistakes are not weaponized, where intentions are clarified rather than assumed, where love is steady and mercy is practiced.

A refuge does not mean the absence of order or accountability. It means the presence of **peace**.

**Peace** that says, *you are safe here.*

**Peace** that says *you are not on trial.*

**Peace** that says, *you are loved, known, and defended.*

This is why the smallest moments matter. A towel on the floor. Clothes on a basket. A tone of voice. A look exchanged. These are not trivial—they are building materials. Used wisely, they strengthen the walls of a home. Used foolishly, they create cracks where resentment and insecurity seep in.

A wise woman builds a house where her husband does not brace himself before walking through the door. Where outsiders quickly learn that your home is not a stage for performance, but a place of rest. Where hospitality flows naturally because peace already lives there.

This is the duty of a biblical wife—not perfection, not control, not constant correction—but **faithful construction**.

Brick by brick.

Word by word.

Day by day.

Creating an atmosphere of peace, hospitality, and order that reflects God's beauty and truth.

Creating a refuge.

Becoming *the* safe place to fall.

*Biblical Womanhood Lived Without Apology*

◆◆◆

## REFOCUSE: Doctrine/Truth

Biblical womanhood is not a cultural construct— it is a covenant calling. A wife's daily duties flow from grace, not guilt; from love, not legalism. Each act of obedience— whether in prayer, service, or submission— is a reflection of her worship toward God and her love for her husband.

## REPRIORITIZE: Action/Obedience

- Duty to Worship
- Duty to the Word
- Duty to Prayer and Intercession
- Duty to Her Home
- Duty to Her Husband
- Duty to Her Children (or Spiritual Children)
- Duty to Serve the Body of Christ
- Duty to Steward Herself
- Duty to Speak Life
- Duty to Reflect Christ in All Things.

**THE BOTTOM LINE:**

Biblical duty is not bondage—it is freedom rightly ordered.

When a woman embraces her God-given duties, she is not shrinking; she is standing firmly in the place God designed her to flourish. Duty does not diminish love— it protects it. It guards the marriage from drift, the home from chaos, and the heart from deception.

Obedience is not cold or mechanical; it is covenantal and alive. Each faithful act—seen or unseen—becomes an offering of worship to God and a tangible expression of love toward her husband and family.

A woman called to duty is a woman anchored in grace, walking in purpose, and building a legacy that honors the Lord.

**REFLECT: Journal Prompts**

- In which area of my daily life do I struggle most to glorify God through obedience?
- How can I better serve and encourage my husband this week?
- Which of these duties requires the most surrender and prayer in this season of my life?
- What Scripture verse can I meditate on to strengthen my walk as a biblical wife?

**RESPOND: Prayer**

*Before I ask You to bless my obedience, I confess where I have resisted authority, withheld respect, or served with resentment instead of joy.*

*Lord, renew my heart and reorder my home. Teach me to walk in Your way as a wife who honors You and blesses her husband. Help me find joy in obedience, peace in service, and purpose in every duty You have entrusted to me. Let my worship begin in the quiet moments and extend through every act of love. Amen.*

# Say What?

*Learning to use my words — without needing to repent after*

*"Set a guard, O Lord, over my mouth; keep watch over the door of*

*my lips!" — Ps. 141:3*

Watching the news the other day, the commentators were absolutely bumfuzzled over a podcast clip where a couple said they had never had an argument. They couldn't believe it.

One even blurted out, "That's unhealthy!"

But here's what they kept circling back to:

"How can anyone live together that long and not disagree?"

And that is where they missed the whole point.

The couple *never* said they had not disagreed.

They said they had never *argued.*

News flash: I have never had an argument with my husband. Not once.

Shocking, I know. Christian Twitter may need a moment.

But Lord knows, I have tried…

Do David and I disagree?

Of course! The man has a brain, and I have one too — and contrary to popular belief, mine does not require batteries, caffeine, or chocolate to function (though those help).

Disagreement is normal. It is healthy. It is part of two redeemed sinners navigating life (and their own sanctification), under one roof.

But arguing? Raising voices? Trading barbs? Weaponizing words?

No.

Not in this house.

Not ever.

Here's what we do instead:

If I disagree with David — especially on something theological — I know what's coming. I'm about to get homework. Not because he's condescending, but because I have a propensity to assume I am correct (I know, try to contain your shock).

So instead of arguing, I will go study. Sometimes I'm right. Sometimes he is. Sometimes we simply agree to disagree and move on with our day — peacefully, lovingly, like two adults who know Christ is watching.

Problem solved. Zero drama. Zero carnage. No emotional crime scene tape required.

Here's why culture doesn't understand this:

They focus on the subject matter. We focus on the subject *that matters* — Our spouse.

If something affects David — whether a person, a problem, or my own poorly timed opinion — the issue is not the issue. The issue is **him**. His heart. His pain. His disappointment. His frustration.

And that is exactly where arguments die before they ever begin.

My role at that moment is not to win. It's to bless. To be soft where he is hurting. To be humble where he is burdened.

To care more about him than about the *thing* that triggered him.

Sometimes that means asking forgiveness — even when I didn't "mean to." (And yes, leaving off the "I didn't mean it" clause because that part only comforts me, not him.)

Sometimes it's simply listening. Sometimes it's reassuring. Sometimes it's silence — the honoring kind, not the punishing kind.

And why do I respond that way?

Because he taught me. Not by lecturing me. Not by managing me. By demonstrating it to me. Every day.

David refuses to engage in conflict that dishonors Christ. No matter how hard my old self used to try.

And here's the truth:

Two people don't accidentally "never argue." You decide it. You build it. You discipline your tongue. You surrender your pride. You crucify the flesh. You pick love over victory. You pick "us" over being right.

Disagreement is inevitable.

The argument is optional.

And peace is the fruit of two people who fear God more than they fear losing an opinion.

*"The beginning of strife is like letting out water, so quit before the quarrel breaks out" (Pr. 17:14).*

Communication is the key to any good relationship. But what exactly do we mean when we say that we need to have good communication skills? Is it all about what you say or is it more like what they hear? What about the tone of our voice or the inflections? What about our body language and how we present ourselves?

We are always communicating. With our words, clothing, our homes, attitudes, and our touch.

We either say, "You are honored and respected," or "You are in the way."

Whether we are communicating through our appearance, our body language, our voice, text messages, our tone, even how we walk… or storm throughout the house… we are communicating something at all times.

One thing I have had to relearn is the ability to effectively communicate. Growing up in my home – words were weapons of warfare – and if not used on the battleground at that moment, the conversation "can and will be used against you" later down the road. Frankly, even some of the so called "Christian" authors and speakers are guilty of word-warfare.

Those different "languages" or "dialects" that you consider near and dear to your heart – and if you don't get love in the "language" you desire then, you don't respond – that's not the sacrificial love that God calls us to– that is sin.

*"Let all that you do be done in love." — 1 Corinthians 16:14*

A woman doesn't just say "I love you"—she lives it.

Love is revealed in tone, in choices, and even in silence. Every look, every word, every task communicates either tenderness or tension. A godly wife is called not just to communicate with her husband, but to communicate about him—what she believes, values, and cherishes.

From what we say, think, wear, read, and do—to how we raise our children and care for our home—we are proclaiming what kind of bride we are.

There are not "languages" of love that are acceptable to respond to, and others we ignore. We would never accept that for ourselves and therefore we cannot ask that of another.

*"Unequal weights and unequal measures are both alike an abomination to the Lord" (Pr. 20:10).*

However, if you know that your beloved loves it when you ___________ fill in the blank, then of course we want to make sure we are "speaking his language." But to expect that (or anything, actually, in return is not the sacrificial love Jesus commands us to express towards others, especially our man).

A couple of years ago, I was in Georgia helping decorate for a baby shower. The whole family was there— everyone except my brother-in-law. When I asked my sister where he was, she casually said he was sick. Then, with a laugh that still makes my stomach turn, she added, *"He can take care of himself. He's a big boy. He knows where the drugs are."*

Mocking. Hateful. Disgusting.

I asked her if she had given him anything to help. She repeated it again— *"He's a big boy. He knows where the drugs are."*

Let me be clear:

That is not strength.

That is not independence.

That is not love.

That is contempt.

A wife does not ridicule her husband in public— especially when he is weak, sick, or vulnerable. Love does not sneer. Covenant does not abandon. And biblical marriage never treats care as optional or compassion as condescending.

Love does not abandon when it's inconvenient.

*"Husbands, love your wives... Wives, see that you respect your husbands" (Eph. 5:25, 33).*

Respect doesn't roll its eyes.

Respect doesn't sneer.

Respect doesn't announce to a room full of people that your husband is on his own.

Marriage is covenantal care, not sarcastic commentary.

A husband is not a roommate.

He is not an inconvenience.

He is not "a big boy" to be dismissed when he's sick.

If a wife cannot be a refuge in her husband's weakness, she is not building a home—she is tearing it down with her own hands (Proverbs 14:1).

Biblical love shows up.

Biblical love covers.

Biblical love does not mock.

Full stop.

There is One love. And He is not defined by our emotions toward Him. Love is not a mood or a moment; It is a reflection of Christ's love for us. Therefore, it is enduring and steadfast through every circumstance and every change of life. Scripture gives us only one definition of love:

*"God is love." — 1 John 4:7*

He is the Author, Creator, and Perfecter of all that love truly is. Therefore, love is not a feeling we chase but a decision we make. It is a conscious, deliberate, and intentional act of the will—rooted in God's character, not our emotions. Feelings may accompany love, but they do not define it.

Real love, as modeled by Christ, is sacrificial, faithful, and enduring—even when feelings fade, circumstances shift, or people fail.

The late great Dr. Voddie Baucham Jr put it this way:

> "Love is an act of the will accompanied by emotion that leads to action on behalf of its object."[3]

True love isn't passive—it moves. It acts. It serves. Love isn't about chasing emotions or getting our way – or in our *preferred* love language; it is about giving our all for the other person, even when we get absolutely nothing in return.

Think about that for a moment… We recite the Scripture, "Love like Jesus" – but we never count the cost of His love for us – His life. If we truly love like Jesus – then we give Him all we've got.

Got it! Great, now tell your face.

**What We Say: Words That Build, Not Break**

*"Gracious words are like a honeycomb, sweetness to the soul and health to the body" (Pr. 16:24).*

Your husband hears more than your tone—he hears your theology. When we honor our husbands in public, we proclaim to the world what we believe about God's design for men. When we dishonor them, even in jest, we tear down our homes with our own hands (Pr. 14:1).

---

[3] Baucham, V. (2007). Family driven faith: Doing what it takes to raise sons and daughters who walk with God. Crossway.

**Heart-Check:**

Do I speak well of my husband to friends, our children, and others?

Do my words give him confidence to lead?

Do I protect his dignity even when I'm frustrated?

Since we communicate on some level every moment of every day, it is important to note that men and women are different. As a woman, we communicate to ourselves as much as we do with others – My husband has a very valid point whenever I ask him if he heard me to respond with, "I didn't know you were talking to me."

## What We Think: Our Internal Conversations Matter

*"As a man thinketh in his heart, so is he…" (Pr. 23:7).*

What we think about our husband becomes what we feel, what we expect, and how we act. Renew your mind (Rom. 12:2) by focusing on what is true, lovely, and commendable (Phil. 4:8). Bitterness begins in the mind before it reaches the mouth.

Ask Yourself:

Do I meditate on his strengths more than his weaknesses?

Do I rehearse offenses or release them through prayer?

Do I discuss the "offenses" with my husband?

Do I believe the best or assume the worst?

The verbal and non-verbal communication is based on and displayed by our expectations and desires of the target audience. We also communicate based on presuppositions of what has been taught to us, either verbal or what we watch on television, read on a blog, or listen to on a podcast. This influences what we have chosen to believe about ourselves and others. That is where the "I know what you meant…" comes from. Presuppositions are your cross to bear and are usually what make you cross and a bear. So, prepare to lay that cross at THE cross and move on.

**What We Read: Feeding the Heart, Shaping the Soul**

You are what you consume. If romance novels or emotionally charged wife groups are fueling discontent or unbiblical expectations, you're not just feeding your emotions— you're poisoning your covenant.

**Nourishment Ideas:**

Read Proverbs 31, Titus 2, and Ephesians 5 often.

Choose books and mentors who inspire faithfulness, not feminism.

As women, we are simply different. A man will go outside, mow the lawn, come inside shower, shave, eat, watch TV and never say a word about the 15 minutes he spent talking to the neighbor about his new riding lawn mower.

We, women, on the other hand, will walk out the door to get the paper out of the driveway and return inside to inform our husband that Joanne and Danny, who live across the street and waved got a new dog (you noticed). And your new next door neighbor Larry was wearing the most beautiful colored yellow shirt…

> "Does he play tennis? I never noticed him wearing a shirt like that."

"Hmmmm."

"He was mowing the lawn on his brand-new riding lawn mower that looked as if it was that new model that you saw down at the Tractor Supply last weekend…Oh! That reminds me, honey, can you please pick up dog food on your way home."

"Mmhmmm… feed the dog after I mow the yard."

"I said he got a new riding lawn mower!"

"Oh, yeah, I saw it, he said that he got it a couple days ago."

"What? When did you talk to Larry?"

Women have been programed to be communicators. Before we came along, God gave Adam the task of naming the animals – God communicated to Adam and Adam responded by completing the task. Adam, being a man, went at the task head on, like the hunter that he is and tackled it. However, you can tell that by the time he got to the birds he was getting tired…  Had that been the task of the woman, I can guarantee we would not have had a "Red," "Blue," "black," or a "Jay…" bird.

Let's face it - we are women. And we do things differently than men do. And that is OK! We can embrace that and live in the freedom of being okay with that fact. We are different.

A woman communicates to express feelings, wants, needs, emotions and desires and we use a lot of words to do so. Men on the other hand, communicate to make a statement… and sometimes they might even use words, but most often not. Sometimes their words… well… are more sounds than words, as observed in the following study:

> Little four-year-old boys and girls were recorded… every noise that came out of their mouths over a period of time.[4]

The study concluded that 100 percent of the sounds made by little girls had something to do with literal words.

> They spent a great deal of time talking to each other, and almost an equal amount of time talking to themselves…[5]

I have learned, over time, that I talk, my husband hears. Sometimes he actually listens, but listening implies that he understands and that is just not always the case. In some circumstances what I am saying does not necessarily require understanding, it does not even require an answer – it simply requires an acknowledgment that I was heard. Because let's face it women talk… a lot!

When I asked my husband to verify this chapter, he laughed at this part.

> "I always listen. I have to. It's the only way to determine if you're talking to me or yourself."

He has a point.

Another study that I read showed that women speak roughly 25,000 words in a day where the average man only speaks 12,000.[6] So

---

[4] Robert Kohn, "Patterns of Hemispheric Specialization in Pre Schoolers," *Neuropsychologia,* 12:505-12.

[5] Gary Smalley and John Trent. *Love is a Decision* (Nashville, TN: Word Publishing, 1989) 44-45.

[6] Ibid. 45

seriously… we cannot be so vain as to think our husbands are going to throw down what they are doing, jump into the thinking position and give us their undivided attention at the mere sound of our sweet voice.

We simply have to understand the fact that we are two completely distinct types of communicators and therefore accept our husbands for who God created them to be: Men. And, according to Kohn, this is how men communicate:

> For little boys, [only] 60 percent [of the noise that came out of their mouths were words. The remaining 40 percent were simply noises and sound effects (like Bzzzzzzzzzzzzz! Zoooooooooooooom! Baaaaammmmmm!).

## What We Wear: Dressing with Honor, Not Competition

*"Strength and dignity are her clothing…" — Proverbs 31:25*

How we dress speaks volumes about how we view our Lord, our husbands, and our marriages. Dress with modesty and beauty—not to compete, manipulate, or blend in with culture, but to communicate that I belong to Him, and I will honor Him (and *h*im) in my appearance.

*"Do not let your adorning be external—the braiding of hair and the putting on of gold jewelry, or the clothing you wear— but let your adorning be the hidden person of the heart with the imperishable beauty of a gentle and quiet spirit, which in God's sight is very precious. For this is how the holy women who hoped in God used to adorn themselves, by submitting to their own husbands…" (1Peter 3:2-6).*

Virgil Walker[7] wrote an amazing piece a year ago. It was geared towards what men need to teach their daughters – But women – we must <u>model</u> this behavior to every woman – young and old, as we are commanded to *"teach the younger women…" (Titus 2:4-6),* and there is no better tool for teaching as our own personal behaviors.

Virgil writes:

- Your body is a temple, not a billboard.

- Modesty is not shame-it's strength under control.

- Your worth isn't found in attention, but in Christ.

- What you wear reveals what you worship.

- Real men don't want what's flaunted-they want what's honored.

- God's design is protection, not punishment.

- The world sells counterfeit beauty, don't buy it.

- Modesty trains the heart to value what God values.

- You represent Christ wherever you go.

- You are not for public consumption-You are God's masterpiece.

*"Husbands, love your wives, as Christ loved the church and gave himself up for her, **that he might sanctify her, having cleansed her by the washing of water with the word, so that he might present the church to himself in splendor, without spot or wrinkle or any such***

---

[7] Virgil Walker serves as a Teaching Pastor at Redeemer Bible Church in Gilbert, Arizona, co-host of the Just Thinking Podcast, and cultural commentator for Jason Whitlock's Podcast Fearless with Blaze Media

***thing, that she might be holy and without blemish***" *(Eph. 5:25-27,*

*emphasis mine).*

Our husbands have been entrusted with a sacred charge—not only to provide and protect, but to shepherd our souls with Christlike love, that we might be presented holy and blameless before the Lord (Eph 5:25–27). This is no light burden. As wives, let us walk in humility and holiness, seeking not to hinder their calling but to strengthen it. May our conduct be marked by gentleness, prayerfulness, and honor, so that in their labor for our sanctification, they find not resistance but refreshment. Let us be, by God's grace, one less care for them to carry—and instead, a crown of joy in their faithful pursuit of Christ.

**What We Do: Homemaking as Honor**

*"She looks well to the ways of her household..."* — *Proverbs 31:27*

One of the most tragic cultural shifts in the past fifty years has been the devaluation of homemaking. Once regarded as one of the highest and most honorable callings, the role of wife, mother, and keeper of the home has been dismissed, mocked, and even scorned.

Women who once were honored, respected, and revered for their unique and vital contributions are now pressured to compete on the same terms as men, as if distinct roles mean unequal worth.

Homemaking is not a consolation prize for women who didn't achieve worldly success—it is a divinely appointed ministry. In God's economy, there is no higher calling than building the home as a sanctuary for worship, discipleship, and refuge.

When a woman prepares a meal, she is not just feeding stomachs—she is nourishing souls.

Laundry isn't just about clothes, it's about covenants. Meal prep is not just nourishment, it's nurture. I am amazed at the number of women who do not cook for their husbands. No breakfast, no lunch – no opportunity to kiss him before he leaves or tell him that he is loved and appreciated in order to get his day going.

The excuses are understandable, but totally invalid.

Sorry ladies.

*"She rises while it is yet night and provides food for her household –*
*Prov. 31:15.*

Get out of bed. Cook your husband's breakfast. Fix his lunch. Take out the meat you will prepare for dinner. (And if your children are home, do the same for them).

I realize that sometimes things happen – I get it. But do not make it the norm for your beloved to fix his own meals. My husband doesn't even fix his own plate.

Every act of service communicates: You matter. This home matters. You matter. Our family matters. No one can communicate this better than his perfect helper. You.

When she creates beauty, she reflects the very nature of the God who created Eden.

**Virtuous Homemaking:**

- Mirrors God's creation of order out of chaos (Gen. 1)

- Cultivates hospitality and joy (Rom. 12:13)

- Trains up children in truth and love (Prov. 22:6)

- Blesses her husband with peace and strength (Prov. 31:11-12)

Every dish scrubbed, every diaper changed, every bed made with love is a silent act of worship—a daily reminder that she is working unto the Lord (Col. 3:23). Homemaking is not trivial. It is sacred.

Let the world mock. Let the culture degrade the role. But let the women of God rise up and reclaim the home as holy ground.

Let some dude put on a dress and think for one minute he can be a woman - Okay, sweetie. Let's see you wake up four times in the night to soothe a baby, then get up before dawn to prep homeschool, clean the kitchen, iron his shirt, train the toddlers in righteousness, text your husband encouragement, fold a mountain of laundry, manage the budget, dress modestly and attractively, get dinner on the table before six, and still look like you slept a full night through and are totally rested and ready for the night ahead!

You don't become a woman by tucking and twirling.

You become a woman only by God's divine design and a biblical woman by dying to yourself, submitting to the Lord, and building a house with wisdom while the world mocks and Satan seethes.

**How We Parent: Showing Him That He is Respected.**

*"She opens her mouth with wisdom, and the teaching of kindness is on her tongue" (Pr. 31:26).*

When you parent with consistency and honor, especially in front of your children, not only are you "training up [your] children in the way they should go," but you elevate your husband's authority and teach your children "to honor their father." Undermining him isn't just bad parenting, it is emasculation and it is covenant sabotage.

As women we do not fully realize the influence and overall impact that we have on our families and on society as a whole. We are not just to teach them to how to live life, but our lives are to be an example. I tell young women everywhere – If you want to know how a man is going to treat you, watch carefully how he treats his mother. Young men will treat their wives the same way they have seen their mother treated and as they grow, they will either respect her or disrespect her based on what she has allowed others to do and say to her and about her.

We have a responsibility to ourselves and our children – not to mention God – who has presented us as a gift to men and therefore, this world. It is imperative that our daughters see and model godly behaviors to emulate and that our boys have a direct reflection of not only biblical womanhood but also taught how they are to treat women.

Few people realize it, but the number one form of domestic abuse is sibling-to-sibling violence. In a research paper I wrote several years ago, I found that many parents minimize harmful dynamics between their children, dismissing them as mere "sibling rivalry"—a misjudgment that can setup a lifelong, damaging trajectory. The ripple effects show up in our broader culture: in how men treat women, and in how women not only allow themselves to be treated, but how they treat men, their children, and other women.

However, the Bible makes it clear that a man who cannot control his children has no place leading the church (1Tim. 3:4-5). Even though Proverbs 31:23 says that your husband "shall be known (respected) in the gates."

Women, this is our huge responsibility. We cannot minimize it, justify it, or excuse it. We must execute it – Biblically.

Since it is only logical that the very first relationship your child will form is with his or her siblings, then you will see why the Bible is so demanding that we "teach our children in the way they should go" (Prov. 22:6) – because your children's behaviors are a direct reflection of how you behave towards one another behind the closed doors of your home.

 As daughters of the Lord our God (Rom 8:17), we bear His *name*, His *authority*, and His *design*. That means we do not accept disrespect or manipulation in our homes—not from children, spouses, or ourselves.

Establishing boundaries that insist on respect is not selfish—it is holy. It teaches our children that:

- *Authority is from God (Rom 13:1)*

- *Honor is due where honor is due (Exod 20:12)*

- *Women are not doormats but image-bearers (Gen 1:27)*

This includes rejecting speech that degrades, controlling patterns, or emotional passivity that allows chaos to fester. A woman who remembers she is the "queen of her husband's heart" (*Song of Solomon 4:7, 6:9*) also remembers that queens do not cower, manipulate, or harbor bitterness—they rule in gentleness and strength, under the Lordship of Christ.

**Children Learn by Watching: The Power of Modeled Love**

*"Be imitators of me, as I am of Christ." — 1 Corinthians 11:1*

Children are born imitators. What they see between their parents becomes their moral framework for:

- Handling conflict
- Understanding roles and respect
- Expressing (or suppressing) love and truth

Children learn relational ethics not only from discipline, but through modeled behavior. If mothers consistently undermine their husbands in tone, sarcasm, or dismissive speech, children learn to do the same. If they watch a mother honor her husband while maintaining her own dignity, they internalize mutual respect. This becomes the seedbed for how they'll treat their siblings now—and their spouses later.

This is why setting boundaries matters. Not only are you guarding your heart (Prov 4:23), but you are also training the next generation of covenant-keepers.

On a side note, just something to keep in mind… If you *really* want to know how that couple in church *truly* feel about you – watch the reaction of their children as you approach to greet them.

**How We Serve: Living Out Submission**

*"Yield now and be at peace with Him; Thereby good will come to you"* *(Job 22:21).*

Godly submission is not servitude; it is sacred strength under God's authority. It is not about becoming less—it is about reflecting Christ.

Submission, properly understood, is not a man wielding power but a woman yielding to the order of God's design.

Christ submitted to the Father in love (John 6:38). The Church submits to Christ in trust (Eph. 5:24). A godly wife submits to her husband not because he is perfect—but because Christ is. This kind of submission empowers a husband to lead in love, to serve with sacrifice, and to be held accountable before God.

Submission Looks Like:

- Trusting God with your husband's leadership.
- Speaking truth in love, not fear.
- Respecting his role even when you don't agree with every decision.

Submission is not silence, it is strength that refuses to manipulate, control, or withhold. It means you honor his God-given role as head of the home, even when your own flesh wants to lead.

*"For the husband is the head of the wife even as Christ is the head of the church, his body, and is himself its Savior" (Eph. 5:23).*

Submission is not weakness—it's strength under the control of Christ. When we serve with joy, not resentment, we showcase the gospel. Every meal, every embrace, every act is sacred when done in the name of Christ. Submission is not a burden. It is our blessing. It is the image of Christ on the cross for our sins – and it is our witness of the representation of Christ and His bride.

**How We Carry Ourselves: Tone, Posture, and Pace**

*"Let your adorning be the hidden person of the heart…"* — *1 Peter 3:4*

In Scripture, modesty is never about frumpiness or shame—it's about *glory-directed presentation.* That means we must reject both:

- Immodest glamour (which demands attention through exposure), and
- Negligent appearance (which dishonors God's image through disorder and disrespect).

Women who arrive at church dressed in a way that suggests sloppiness, uncleanliness, or "homelessness" (disheveled, careless, or disengaged) send a signal—whether intended or not—that God is not worthy of effort, and His people are not worthy of respect.

Both extremes distort worship.

## A THEOLOGY OF DIGNITY: CHRIST-CENTERED SELF-PRESENTATION

God does not call women to dress in designer labels. He calls them to dress with *discernment and dignity.*

*"Adorn themselves in respectable apparel, with modesty and self-control."* — *1 Timothy 2:9*

Let's break that down:

- Respectable: appropriate, thoughtful, and intentional
- Modesty: not drawing attention to the body sexually
- Self-control: not indulgent, reactive, or careless

So yes—the women who dress as if they rolled out of bed or out of a tent, with no sense of sacred presence, are not honoring the God of beauty and order. This isn't about class or fashion—it's about *reverence.*

## MODESTY IS NOT MIDDLE-CLASS – IT'S CHRISTLIKE

Some women will say, "I don't have much to wear," or, "God looks at the heart." True—but the heart *shapes the effort.*

- You don't need wealth to be clean.
- You don't need trends to be presentable.
- You don't need glamor to be *godly.*

As daughters of the King, we are representatives of Christ. That means:

- We don't draw attention to our bodies through exposure.
- We don't repel through chaos and neglect.
- We *present ourselves with joyful reverence* in the presence of God.

*"For God is not a God of confusion but of peace... Let all things be done decently and in order."* — *1 Corinthians 14:33, 40*

That includes how we dress and how we carry our bodies.

## FINAL CALL: DIGNITY, NOT DISORDER

The church is a *household of the living God* (1 Tim 3:15). Our dress and demeanor should reflect that truth. Whether married or single, rich or poor, new believer or mature saint—every Christian woman should be asking:

- Does my appearance say I fear the Lord?

- Am I putting in thoughtful effort, or am I drawing attention (positive or negative) to myself?
- Would I dress like this to meet a king?

Because you already are.

*"You shall be called Hephzibah... for the Lord delights in you." —* Isaiah 62:4

## MODESTY FLOWS INTO MANNER: THE POSTURE OF OUR PRESENCE

Biblical modesty doesn't end with fabric—it flows through *how* we carry ourselves.

Once we've dressed in a way that reflects reverence, we must ask: Does the rest of me—the way I walk, speak, and interact—match the holiness I claim to wear?

*"Let your adorning be the hidden person of the heart..." — 1 Peter 3:4*

**Because body language says what our mouths won't.**

- Eye rolls, dismissive glances, sarcasm, sighs—these don't just "express mood," they *communicate contempt.*
- But a warm smile, a pause to listen, a thoughtful text during the day, a gentle touch—they preach something better: "I cherish you. I love you. I want you."

This is especially vital in our marriages and in front of our children. They're watching not just what we say, but *how we say it.* Our tone, posture, and presence reveal what kind of spirit rules our hearts.

*"From the abundance of the heart the mouth speaks." — Matthew 12:34*

And the body *moves*.

So we must ask: Is my body—my tone, my expressions, my posture—aligned with the Spirit of Christ or the spirit of the age?

*Learning to use my words — without needing to repent after*

◆◆◆

**REFOCUS: Doctrine/Truth**

Words are never neutral.

Every word, tone, glance, silence, and sigh is either building your marriage or tearing it down. Scripture is unambiguous: *"Death and life are in the power of the tongue" (Pr. 18:21).* That includes the words spoken out loud, the ones typed with thumbs, and the ones rehearsed silently in the heart.

Biblical communication is not about self-expression — it is about stewardship. A wife's words are entrusted to her by God to cultivate peace, safety, desire, and honor in her home. When her speech is governed by the Spirit, her mouth becomes a place of refuge. When it is governed by the flesh, it becomes a weapon.

Your husband does not just hear your words — he lives under them.

To "say what?" is to ask a better question:

Does what I say — and how I say it — reflect Christ, honor my husband, and protect our covenant?

**REPRIORITIZE: Action/Obedience**

**Pray For Your Husband.**

- Scripture-saturated prayer is one of the most intimate ways to communicate love. It aligns your heart with God's will for him and opens your eyes to his needs.

- Greet Him Face to Face

- Meet him at the door. Make eye contact. Let him know his arrival matters – and maybe even do it naked.

**Make Words Count**

Put the phone down. Speak with purpose. Listen to understand, not to defend. Send a note in his lunch. Take a dry eraser marker and write I "heart" you on his bathroom mirror, tuck a note in his sock drawer for him to find later.

**Make a Direct Impact**

Kiss him like you mean it. Hold his hand on purpose. Serve with joy.

Let God Change the Way You Think: Surrender your checklist. Seek first the kingdom. Let the Spirit sanctify your priorities. Your husband is your FIRST ministry. You were created for his glory (1 Cor. 11:7).

Present yourself like you belong to the King of kings.

And teach your children to do the same.

**THE BOTTOM LINE:**

You don't need better communication techniques.

You need a renewed mind and a disciplined tongue.

When a wife learns to speak with intention instead of impulse, love replaces tension, trust replaces defensiveness, and repentance becomes rare instead of routine. A woman who governs her words builds a home that feels safe, desired, and respected — not because her husband is perfect, but because her obedience is worship.

You cannot control your husband.

You can control your mouth.

And when your words align with truth, grace, and honor, your marriage begins to reflect the gospel — loudly, clearly, and without apology.

**REFLECT: Journal Prompts**

- What subtle messages do I send my husband every day?
- What subtle messages am I sending others about my husband through my body language, "prayer requests," social media posts, etc.
- How does my wardrobe reflect (or neglect) my love for him?
- What about my love for Jesus?
- Am I respectful? Honoring?
- Where am I investing more emotional or physical energy than I am in my marriage?
- Am I building him up in front of our children and friends?

**RESPOND: Prayer**

*Before I ask You to change my circumstances, I confess where my words have been careless, critical, defensive, or dishonoring—especially toward my husband.*

*Lord, let my life preach louder than my lips. Teach me to speak love fluently—with my words, my service, my dress, my tone, and my thoughts. Help me reflect You as I love, honor, and cherish the man You gave me. Amen.*

# Faithful Friends or Toxic Influence?

## Spotting the Difference Between Godly Counsel and The Hot Mess Express

*"Do not associate with a babbler" (Pr. 20:19).*

Faith consists of persistent hope in the promises of God. What if you loved your husband by way of faith? That is believing in God's promise of who He says your husband is, rather than who you (or your friends) think your husband is.

After the newness has worn off and the luster is gone… expectations can begin to creep in. Ideas of what we feel "should be" rears their ugly heads and the door swings open to disappointment, dissatisfaction, frustration, and failure. Suddenly that man of our dreams has become that man we want to change. Not only does he not do the right things, but he also does not say the right things, act the right way or even look right. And maybe he doesn't. But that does not negate your responsibility to love him, obey him, honor him and respect him.

After all, you married him and not only is he God's chosen one for you. He is a direct reflection of your choices. You did in fact say, "I do." Therefore, you do. You can do. You must do. You will do.

"Do" is a verb. It is an action word. It means get on it (that is my interpretation, by the way) Take action. Make something happen.

So, you can tell me and others how much you love your husband, but if you are not actively loving your husband, your words are "only a resounding gong or a clanging cymbal"[8] and mean nothing. Your actions speak louder than your words will ever speak:

*"So also faith by itself, if it does not have works, is dead. But someone will say, "You have faith and I have works." Show me your faith apart from your works, and I will show you my faith by my works. You believe that God is one; you do well. Even the demons believe and shudder! Do you want to be shown, you foolish person, that faith apart from works is useless? Was not Abraham our father justified by works when he offered up his son Isaac on the altar? You see that faith was active along with his works, and faith was completed by his works; and the Scripture was fulfilled that says, "Abraham believed God, and it was counted to him as righteousness"—and he was called a friend of God. You see that a person is justified by works and not by faith alone"* (Js. 2:17-25).

**How Do You "*Do?*"**

---

[8] Holy Bible 1 Cor. 13:1

Start with friendship. Abraham was called a friend of God. Friends are vital. We were made for relationship—with God and with one another, starting with your spouse.

And do it, unapologetically.

A few years ago, we had a high school reunion and I met up with some old classmates for lunch. It was in an area of town that was newly developed and my husband and I had never been, so I asked him to come with me and drop me off and then we could meet up later, after my lunch, and see what was all new in that part of town.

But the moment I walked in and said hello, one of my oldest and what I thought was a dear friend, said, "Oh! I'm so glad your husband let you come!"

I just looked at her and shook my head.

What? Why?

What I wanted to say was, *"I'm sorry your husband doesn't want to be seen in public with you."*

After all, he was nowhere to be found at the reunion and if you scour her social media, you might see an old photo of their wedding, but that's about it. Lots and lots of her and her two daughters… and her "church" friends.

But I tamed my tongue, silently evaluated our relationship, and pretended she didn't mean it *that way*. After all, David had literally dropped me off – where was I going to go?

That moment told me everything I needed to know.

Some women don't want freedom—they want validation for their rebellion. And some friendships don't strengthen covenant—they resent it.

A woman who mocks, minimizes, or misunderstands your marriage will *always* try to reframe your faithfulness as control and your joy as submission gone wrong. What she calls "concern" is often just contempt dressed up in Christian language.

Wise women pay attention to that.

Scripture warns us that *"bad company corrupts good morals"* (1 Corinthians 15:33). And that corruption doesn't always look loud or hostile—it often sounds like sarcasm, subtle digs, and comments meant to make you question whether honoring your husband is something you should be embarrassed about.

It is not.

That lunch didn't end a friendship. It clarified one. And clarity, while sometimes uncomfortable, is a gift of discernment.

Not every woman who has access to your life deserves influence in it.

Scripture is not silent about influence. Psalm 1 warns us that blessing is found not in *walking in the counsel of the wicked*, nor *standing in the way of sinners*, nor *sitting in the seat of scoffers*— and scoffing often sounds like subtle mockery of God's design, not open rebellion.

Titus 2 further instructs older women to train younger women in self-control, reverence, and faithfulness in marriage, *so that the word of God may not be reviled*. When women belittle covenant obedience, frame honor as oppression, or mock marital unity under the guise of concern or humor, they are not offering friendship—they are offering counsel that erodes faith.

A wise woman discerns her circle carefully, knowing that she cannot grow rooted like a tree planted by streams of water while sitting at tables that quietly scoff at what God has declared good.

The Hebrew root words for friendship—*r'h* (companion) and *'hb* (affection, devotion)—show the depth of what real friendship means. Friends are not just companions; they are counsel, refuge, accountability, and spiritual encouragement. A godly friend rebukes in love, rejoices in blessing, and prays without ceasing.

Cultivate your marriage like a garden. Plant kindness. Pull weeds of bitterness. Water your husband with grace and joy. Believe Philippians 1:6—that God will complete the good work He started in both of you.

Too many women know their girlfriends better than they know their own husbands. They share hopes, dreams, favorite stories and, too often, gossip. Especially about their husbands. That is unacceptable. Gossip is sin, and when it targets your spouse, it tears down your home (Prov. 14:1).

If you are not a refuge for your husband, you're a liability. 1 Peter 5:8 reminds us: Be sober-minded; be watchful. Your adversary the devil prowls around like a roaring lion. He doesn't attack Adam until Eve enters the scene—and marriage becomes the battlefield.

Make Him Your True BFF.

BUT PLEASE! Do not expect your husband to be your girlfriend. He is not.

Stop assigning feminine expectations to a man God made for leadership and strength. No, he will not chat like your BFF. No, more than likely he is not going to analyze your stories with the same depth as your girlfriends. But he was given to you by God to be your protector, provider, and most importantly: Your life partner/partner for life.

So set down the assumptions. Stop reading into his body language. Don't try to mind-read. Speak plainly, love kindly, and remember he was never meant to replace your girlfriends—he was meant to be your covenant companion.

In the book *Real Marriage*, it is stated straightforwardly: "Husbands and wives who want their marriages to be enduring and endearing must be friends."[9] John Gottman adds: "Happy marriages are based on deep friendship… friendship fuels the flames of romance."[10]

And that is exactly what we are here to do – fan those flames!

Yes, you are different. And that's the point. But those differences should be complemented, not a competition. Female friends are fine—as long as they don't replace your husband or put him (by way of you, especially), in compromising positions.

---

[9] Mark Driscoll and Grace Driscoll, Real Marriage: The Truth about Sex, Friendship, and Life Together (Nashville: Thomas Nelson, 2012). *NOTE: this is not an endorsement for Mark Driscoll.*
[10] John Gottman, The Seven Principles for Making Marriage Work (New York: Three Rivers Press, 1999).

Never make your husband have to "explain" your behavior. Let your integrity give him rest.

Where you go, what you do, and who you are with—these things count. They reflect on you, your husband, your family, the bride of Christ, and more importantly, on the One you call, Lord.

I will also take this opportunity to add that if you are gossiping about your husband to others – then you must repent of that sin and realize that you are not providing your husband the safe and secure home that God calls you to provide to him and you are putting your marriage in danger:

*"The heart of her husband <u>trusts</u> in her" (Proverbs 31:11a).*

Even when he is not with her…

I know the first thing that women will say is that they are different then their spouse. Joe has his friends that he does things with and Sally has her friends that she does things with and that all relationships are different. That may be very true and, in some cases, we do have to have those special friends to go and do things with but first and foremost – they cannot replace your husband. And secondly, they must be the same sex.

Friendship demands mutual respect. So, meet him where he is. You love fashion, he loves baseball? Great. Wear something cute to spring training and learn to laugh in the bleachers.

Friendship does not demand sameness—it thrives on service and understanding.

Remember: this book is about _you_ changing how _you_ love _your_ husband—not how he loves you. This is not "I'll scratch your back if you scratch mine."

It is: I will be faithful—even if he never changes or responds. Because friendship with your spouse, like love, is covenantal, not contractual.

Larry Crabb said:

> Nothing reaches so deeply into the human personality as relationship… From Genesis to Revelation, the Bible is a story of relationships.[11]

So be faithful. Sit with him during the game. You won't die from watching football – as a matter of fact, you might just learn, like me, that you love baseball and/or football and like me, you might have missed your calling as the best arm-chair football coach, ever!

_"Therefore, humble yourselves under the mighty hand of God, that He may exalt you in due time, casting all your care upon Him, for He cares for you." —1 Peter 5:6–7_

Being a friend to your spouse, no matter how you (silently) might feel about him at any given moment, and no matter if the action is reciprocated… It is your first step in being faithful.

---

[11]Larry Crabb, The Marriage Builder (Grand Rapids, MI: Zondervan, 1982), 192.

## REFOCUS: Doctrine/Truth

Friendship is not optional in marriage—it's foundational. Biblical friendship isn't built on shared hobbies or personalities, but on covenant loyalty, mutual honor, and Spirit-led devotion.

Your husband was never designed to compete with your girlfriends, your family's opinions, or the voices of culture. He is the one flesh partner God gave you, the companion of your covenant, the friend meant to walk beside you in every season (Mal. 2:14).

Your circle matters. Your influences matter.

Where you go, what you do, and who you surround yourself with either strengthens your marriage—or slowly erodes it.

*"Blessed is the man who walks not in the counsel of the wicked... but his delight is in the law of the LORD" (Ps. 1:1–2).*

If you want your marriage to flourish, you must root yourself beside streams of living water—not in circles of scoffers, gossipers, or discontented friends.

Your friendship with your husband is not a bonus to your marriage. It is the heartbeat of it.

**REPRIORITIZE: Action/Obedience**

1. **Make Your Husband Your First Friend.**

   Friendship in marriage must be cultivated, not assumed. Choose connection over convenience. Choose presence over distraction.

   **Do this:** Spend 15 distraction-free minutes a day with him—no phone, no tasks, no agenda. Just be together. (and don't tell him – just do it!)

   I was listening to a podcast one day and I loved what I heard one of the women saying. She explained that her husband enjoyed working off his stress by working on the old car in the garage. She also noticed that when he made his trek outside, their daughter followed him. They had a fantastic father-daughter relationship. So, one day, she decided I need to do that too!

   It is not up to your husband to "schedule" you into his life. Be a part of his. Meet him wherever he is and invite him in to where ever you are.

2. **Guard Your Circle Like Your Marriage Depends on It.**

   Because It Does. Some friendships edify. Others erode. Your heart is shaped by your closest influences, for better or worse.

   **Do this:** Identify one person or influence that consistently fuels discontentment, disrespect, or comparison—and set a boundary this week.

Shut the Door on Gossip — Completely. Talking negatively about your husband is not "processing" it is sin. You are either guarding his dignity or giving it away.

**Do this:** Replace every complaint with a spoken compliment. Speak life to him—not about him.

3. **Enter His World**

Even When It is Not Your World. Friendship grows through shared experiences, not just shared opinions. You do not have to love the activity — you just have to love the man.

**Do this:** Join him in one thing he enjoys this week: the game, the walk, the project, the show.

4. **Silence Competing Voices.**

Your covenant cannot flourish if it competes with the chorus of worldly advice, bitter girlfriends, or discontent-filled feeds.

**Do this:** Conduct a "voice audit." Unfollow, mute, or step back from anything that stirs ingratitude, cynicism, or comparison in your marriage.

5. **Speak Life Into Your Marriage.**

Friendship thrives on words that build trust, safety, and joy.

**Do this:** Tell him one specific thing today that you admire, appreciate, or enjoy about him.

6. **Walk in Integrity**

Your choices—where you go, what you do, who you're with—communicate your loyalty and your honor.
Integrity protects your marriage and glorifies your Lord.

**Do this:** Commit to living above reproach. No questionable relationships. No blurred lines. No secrecy.

7. **Pray for a Friend's Heart**

Ask God for tenderness, affection, patience, and joy toward your husband. Friendship is a work of the Spirit, not merely effort.

**Do this:** Pray over your husband daily—his heart, his leadership, his burdens, his joy, his walk with Christ.

## THE BOTTOM LINE:

Marriage flourishes when friendship is protected, prioritized, and pursued. Your husband should never feel like he has to compete with friends, family, or outside voices for your loyalty or affection.

When you cultivate friendship in your marriage— real, joyful, intentional friendship— you are building your home, guarding your covenant, and reflecting the steadfast love of Christ.

Friendship is not extra. It is essential.

And it begins with you.

## REFLECT: Journal Prompts

- Do I treat my husband as a companion or a competitor?

- In what ways have I allowed others—friends, family, or media—(including those romance novels you need to lay at the foot of the cross), to influence how I think about him?

- Am I allowing the women I listen to—and the words I entertain—to train me toward greater reverence, self-control, and faithfulness in my marriage, or are they quietly teaching me to scoff at what God calls good?

- If a younger woman were watching my friendships and listening to my conversations, would she be learning to honor her future husband—or to undermine him?

- Do I gossip about my husband or guard his dignity in every conversation?

- Have I made time to enjoy my husband's interests, even when they don't align with mine?

- Am I building a friendship with him—or expecting him to act like my girlfriends?

- What expectations do I need to release so I can better love him?

- How can I intentionally cultivate friendship in my marriage this week?

**RESPOND: Prayer**

*Before I ask You for peace, I confess where I have allowed ungodly counsel, comparison, or fear of people to shape my thinking.*

*Lord, make me a faithful friend to my husband. Teach me to protect, nurture, and delight in our friendship. Let me value our differences as gifts, not inconveniences. May my words build, my loyalty comfort, and my presence be a blessing in his life. Shape me into a wife who reflects Your steadfast love—steadfast in every season, faithful in every friendship. Amen.*

# Chapter Sex: ...Uhhhh Six:

## Naked and Unashamed

*Side Note (but an important one): This chapter is **<u>not</u>** written for those walking through domestic or sexual violence.*

*As someone who has spent over four decades advocating for survivors and leading healing ministry, I know the weight and trauma of abuse — and I hold it with reverence. If you've experienced domestic violence, sexual assault, or coercion — or if pornography, orgies, or any kind of "third-party fantasy" has crept into your marriage — this chapter <u>(this book) is NOT for you.</u> Those are not things that add "spice" — they are sin, and abuse. Period. And I've created an entire separate ministry to help you walk through that healing journey: <u>CrossStrengthMinistries.org</u>.*

---

Now — back to those of you who are in a biblical, God-honoring marriage and your love life has, well… let's just say the pilot light's on, but dinner is cold.

You love your husband. He loves you. But somewhere between the kids, the calendar, and the 37-throw pillows on your bed, intimacy has turned into a handshake and a shared sleep schedule.

**This chapter is especially for you.**

We're going to talk about how sex in marriage is not just allowed — it's celebrated in Scripture.

Not gross. Not taboo. Not shameful. God invented it. And when it's enjoyed inside His design, it's not only "okay" — it's holy, healing, and really, really fun.

*"And the man and his wife were both naked and were not ashamed"*
*(Gen. 2:25).*

The number of times I have read right over the top of this Scripture is innumerable. But one day it caught my attention and drew me in to take a deeper look as to what that "naked and unashamed," meant and to see if it was something that could ever be recaptured in a marriage.

Especially when there was someone in that marriage as broken as me.

As a child, I was abandoned by my biological father, abused by my stepfather, molested by my step-grandfather – and if that wasn't enough, I was gang-raped by the teenage boy and his four friends that lived next door to my grandparents.

But I think what lingered in my heart for so long was being emotionally abandoned by my mother who told to not to mention the molestation or abuse or there would be consequences. I grew up being further abused and like a good little girl, I kept my mouth shut. As time went by, I felt dirty, unworthy, and very ashamed. Later I would go on to encounter a date rape and an unrelated abortion. By the time I was thirty I had been married and divorced three times and raised two children on my own while making my living as a stripper.

To be "naked" emotionally or otherwise in my marriage – especially to a man after God's own heart, like David – was not an option for me – I would never again open myself up to anyone for any reason ever, I thought – But actually, it was the exact opposite.

Desperate for love (in all the wrong places), Obviously, I literally dumped Dave at the alter… I opened myself up to more shame, guilt and ridicule – because I was in unholy relationships with abusive men, all of which were addicted to pornography – just like the ones I grew up with.

So, when David came back into my life, I honestly did not know what to make of him. I certainly did not know how to answer his first question: "So, what have you been up to for the past 25 years…"

He was so different, so loving and so kind that I ran away like that scarred little girl – just knowing that when he found out all that I had been through (when I got emotionally naked) – he would leave me (shame me), just like everyone had done throughout my life.

But biblical intimacy isn't just about sex. It's about security. To be naked and unashamed is to be known — fully, honestly, raw and real.

It is the gospel lived out in the covenant of marriage.

It is not just allowing yourself to be seen. It is also choosing to see your spouse through the lens of who God says they are — not through the lens of past pain or imperfections.

That is the kind of love that changes everything.

And let me tell you. It is a welcome change!

Today, I know I'm blessed. God brought David back into my life 25 years after I first ran from him. And he calls me a gift — still.

I know me. I know the mess I used to be. But that's not who I am anymore. And it most certainly isn't how He sees me.

There was a time I held onto everything. I remembered every offense, every failure, storing it up like ammunition in case I needed to protect myself. No one could be "naked" in front of me, because I was constantly keeping score.

What finally changed was this realization: Scripture <u>never once</u> tells me to forgive *myself*.

My sin is mine. My failures are mine. My shameful decisions belong to me—not so I can punish myself, but so I never forget how easily my heart turns when left unchecked. Without that awareness, humility erodes and pride creeps in quietly, convincing me I'm safer than I actually am.

God has forgiven me—fully and finally—through Christ. That is settled. But remembering what I am capable of apart from Him keeps me watchful, dependent, and honest. It dismantles the need to self-protect and exposes the illusion of control.

And only when that illusion is broken can I stop keeping score—long enough to choose trust over fear.

After years of failed relationships and surface-level connections, I realized I had to stop holding my beloved responsible for every sin that I had done or that had been done against me. And I made a decision: Would I keep fearing people, or would I start believing God?

It wasn't easy.

> *"I slept, but my heart was awake. A sound! My beloved is knocking. 'Open to me, my sister, my love, my dove, my perfect one...'" (Song 5:2).*

I hear that knock in the hearts of women I talk to. We all want intimacy. We all want connection. But most of us have no idea how to actually be *naked and unashamed.*

We see our flaws. Every past mistake (that we have done or that has been done to us). Every wrinkle, stretch mark, every sagging place where gravity has done its job. And as the years pass, the "mood lighting" gets dimmer, and we start changing clothes in the closet. We hide in the dark and ask our husbands to imagine who we used to be.

Intimacy fades.

When I blog about this, I get interesting responses.

Some are excuses disguised as theology. Others are from frustrated, emasculated men begging their wives to open that proverbial door, just like Solomon with his bride.

> Comment from SB #1: "Holly, this feels very judgmental! There are times when God says the two should separate! Like after childbirth or with serious health issues."

My response: Of course, there's grace. But do not twist Scripture. That passage also says to separate only for a mutual time of prayer. Are you praying? Or avoiding?

Comment from LC #2 (a husband): "Want your wife to be intimate? Do the dishes. Clean the bathrooms. Change the sheets."

My response: That's performance-based sex. And no, ladies — that is not biblical. Sex is not a transaction. It's not a prize for chores well done. That mindset isn't just emasculating; it's manipulative. And in some cases, it crosses the line into sexual control.

Let's be honest. We have an arsenal of excuses:

I'm tired.

I just showered.

I'm in my jammies.

The kids are awake.

I didn't shave.

Yep. Me too.

And we're not the first:

*"I had put off my garment; how could I put it on? I had bathed my feet; how could I soil them?" (Song 5:3).*

We've been dodging intimacy since ancient times.

But God didn't design sex to be a horrid duty or a dread. He designed it to be healing, joyful, affirming, holy — and sometimes, even spicy. But only when we're willing to be both: naked and unashamed.

When writing this chapter, I thought that the most important, well-informed individual I could ask about being naked and unashamed, would be my beloved. I didn't want to put him on the spot – or embarrass him – I wanted honest answers that would require thought.

So, I sent him a text message.

> Think about me standing right in front of you, naked.... tell me:
>
> 1. What do you see?
> 2. What do you think?
> 3. What do you feel?

And then I waited.

> 1. Intimacy, vulnerability, perfection.
> 2. Secure, loved, cherished.
> 3. God is good! Thank you, Lord!"

But those were the Spiritual answers – I wanted the *real* answers... You know the ones!

So, when he arrived home for lunch – I asked him again, this time I was more specific...

> "Babe," I said, "Your answers were great... But…" (Big sexy-smile) "I'm looking for a little more than that..." I continued.

Honestly, he looked a little worried.

Then he said, "boobs!"

I said: "Let me help you... When I look in the mirror I see age spots, pudgy tummy, squishy butt, one saggy boob, and unshaved legs... Hardly something worth viewing in the light of day – let alone as foreplay."

He laughed.

"I'm not taking inventory! I'm looking at my hot naked wife and thinking, 'Thank you Jesus!'"

And then He continued:

"Honestly babe, I don't look at you like that – I see my beautiful wife that I love and feel that same vulnerability that you feel – I'm not perfect either – we are what we are – and as far as I'm concerned, we're perfectly joined together. When you open yourself up to that same vulnerability – I feel honored that you trust me to just love you and cherish you – in all your glory! I put my focus on the beauty that you are – inside and out... I see my perfect wife."

Taking his plate of taco salad and heading to the living room, he continued:

"By the way - To tell you the truth, I couldn't tell you when, or if you have *ever* shaved your legs..."

To put my husband's thoughts in the words of Jeff Foxworthy: What are men thinking? "I'd like a beer and I'd like to see something naked" (Totally Committed, 1998).

Men are really quite that simple.

*"Awake, O north wind, and come, O south wind! Blow upon my garden, let its spices flow. Let my beloved come to his garden and eat its choicest fruits" (Song 4:16)*

I got news for you girlie – Solomon's wife ain't making no fruit-tart!

So, the appropriate answer to the request – is: Yes.

Yep. Sure. Of course. Why not? Indeed! Certainly. Absolutely! YAY! No problem. Okay. I agree!! By all means.

Right here or in the bedroom?

Better yet, don't wait for his leading... Just get naked.

*"The sluggard does not plow in the autumn; he will seek at harvest and have nothing" (Pr. 20:4).*

**Final Thought: Pornography Isn't Just a "Man's Issue"[12]**

Pornography is not a male-only sin. That myth has cost women their holiness and their marriages.

---

[12] **Research Note:** Multiple studies over the past two decades have documented a significant rise in pornography consumption among women, with data indicating that women now represent roughly one-third of all pornography users. Research in psychology and neuroscience has further shown that women are more likely to engage with sexually explicit content through written material, emotionally driven narratives, and fantasy-based media—forms that activate the same reward, arousal, and conditioning pathways in the brain as visual pornography does in men. The medium differs; the effect does not. Lust, regardless of format, conditions desire away from covenant intimacy and toward private gratification.

Research has shown that women are just as entrenched as men — the difference is *how* the sin presents itself. While men often engage visually, women are more likely to engage emotionally and imaginatively. And Scripture makes no distinction between the two.

Romance novels, explicit fiction, and emotionally charged media often serve as pornography for women. They are graphic. They are sexually stimulating. And they cultivate fantasies that are not holy.

These stories do not train a woman to love her husband — they train her to *escape* him. They create imaginary men, fictional intimacy, and unrealistic expectations that no real husband can compete with. And when desire is continually fed outside the covenant, intimacy inside the marriage inevitably starves.

Jesus was unmistakably clear: lust does not require physical touch to be sin. It begins in the heart (Matthew 5:28). Fantasizing about a man who is not your husband — even if he exists only on paper — is a misuse of desire God designed exclusively for the marriage covenant.

This isn't about banning books or policing preferences. It's about guarding holiness. What we consume shapes what we crave. And what we crave will eventually shape how we love — or withhold love — from our husbands.

God designed sexual desire to be *directed*, not dispersed. Romance novels and fantasy-driven content fracture that design by training the heart to respond to stimulation without covenant, intimacy without responsibility, and desire without sacrifice.

Biblical intimacy requires discipline of the mind as much as the body. A woman cannot pursue "naked and unashamed" intimacy with her husband while privately entertaining fantasies that belong nowhere but the imagination.

Holiness is not repression. It is alignment. And when desire is rightly ordered — protected, guarded, and directed toward one man — intimacy becomes deeper, safer, and far more satisfying than any counterfeit the world offers.

What you secretly feed will eventually starve your marriage.

*Marriage is to be held in honor among all, and the marriage bed is to be undefiled; for fornicators and adulterers God will judge*

*(Heb. 13:4, NASB)*[13]

---

[13] New American Standard Version, (1995).

**REFOCUS: Doctrine/Truth**

Shame is a liar.

It whispers that you're unworthy, undesirable, unforgivable, and beyond redemption.

But the truth? God sees you through the righteousness of Christ — and if your husband loves Jesus, he likely sees you through that same filter.

*"My dove, my perfect one... beautiful as the moon, bright as the sun" (Song 6:9a, 10b).*

If Scripture tells us not to deprive one another (1 Cor. 7:5), then why do we do it?

Because shame still sneaks in.

Because time and gravity haven't exactly done us favors.

Because we sometimes care more about how _we_ feel than about what God has said.

But the most damaging barrier to intimacy — with God and with our husbands — is unrepented, unresolved sin.

Not just the sins we've committed, but the sins others have committed against us that we've never fully released.

***Here's a fact: People have, will, and will continue to sin against you for the rest of your time on earth. What will you do with that? Will it bring honor to God?*

**REPRIORITIZE: Action/Obedience**

- Let's stop letting past sin, pain, or body shame steal from present intimacy.

- Let's stop using bitterness and self-protection as excuses.

- It's time to get spiritually and emotionally naked — before God and before our husbands.

**Here's how to start:**

- Face the shame — not to wallow in it, but to confess it and be free from it.

- Accept Christ's forgiveness.

- Forgive others — not necessarily to restore the relationship, but to release yourself from their debt.

- Talk to your husband — make restitution if needed. Invite him in, not just to your body, but to your journey.

- Protect your vineyard — identify the "little foxes" (Song 2:15) that keep stealing your joy, your security, and your intimacy.

*"Catch the foxes for us, the little foxes that spoil the vineyards, for our vineyards are in blossom" (Song 2:15).*

**These foxes can be:**

- Past wounds still unhealed

- Expectations rooted in fantasy, not faith

- Cultural lies about beauty, value, or romance

- People who drain, discourage, or distract you from your calling

- Even family can be one of those foxes — honor them, yes. But sometimes, from a healthy distance.

## THE BOTTOM LINE:

- You cannot love fully if you are chained by shame.

- You cannot give yourself freely if you are still holding onto pain that Jesus died to set you free from.

- To be naked and unashamed is not just about physical vulnerability — it is about spiritual courage.

- It's not about having a perfect body. It is about having a perfect Savior.

## REFLECT: Journal Prompts

- What am I still ashamed of from my past? List anything that comes to mind.

- Have I truly accepted Christ's forgiveness for my own sins — or do I still rehearse past guilt as if Christ's blood wasn't enough?

- What am I consuming that stirs desire away from my covenant — and am I willing to surrender it fully to Christ today?

- Ask the Lord to reveal areas where shame or unresolved pain are blocking intimacy.

- Confess past sins you've buried or tried to manage without grace.

- Invite God to help you forgive those who've sinned against you—release their debt.

- Pray for honesty, courage, and tenderness in conversations with your husband.

- Ask the Spirit to expose and remove the "little foxes" in your life and marriage.

- Rest in the truth that God sees you as *radiant* in Christ (Eph. 5:27).

## RESPOND: Prayer

Let your prayer be marked by *honesty without fear*. God is not scandalized by your story—He is glorified by your surrender. Bring everything into the light. That is where freedom lives.

If you wrestle with believing you can be truly free from shame, consider this: If Christ's death was sufficient for your salvation, how can it not be sufficient for your healing?

To carry what Christ already carried to the cross is not humility—it is unbelief dressed up as guilt.

> *"The guilt of sin is removed instantly by justification; the stain of sin is washed gradually by sanctification."* – John Owen

*Before I ask You to restore intimacy, I confess where fear, shame, or self-protection has kept me hidden and resistant to Your design.*

*I confess that I have allowed my desires to wander beyond the boundaries You designed for my good. I have consumed words, images, or fantasies that stirred longing apart from covenant, and I acknowledge this as sin — not excusable, not harmless, and not hidden from You.*

*I repent of feeding my imagination what does not honor You or my husband. Cleanse my heart and renew my mind. Retrain my desires so that they are directed, disciplined, and satisfied where You intended — within the safety of marriage and under Your authority.*

*Help me tear down every counterfeit version of intimacy I have tolerated and restore purity, trust, and unity in my marriage. Teach me to bring my whole self — body, mind, and heart — into obedience to Christ.*

*I choose holiness over habit, obedience over indulgence, and covenant over fantasy.*

*You are the One who sees, forgives, and covers Your children in perfect righteousness. You are not ashamed to call us Your own (Heb. 2:11). In You, there is no condemnation—only grace that redeems and restores.*

*Lord, cultivate in me the fruit of humility, honesty, and freedom. Help me to lay down false coverings of pride, shame, or fear, and walk instead in the boldness that comes from being clothed in Christ (Gal. 3:27).*

*In Jesus' name, Amen.*

# Virtue

## Holy but Spicy: The Sanctified Sass of a Virtuous Woman

*"An excellent wife is the crown of her husband, but she who brings shame is like rottenness in his bones," (Pr. 12:11).*

*"...Make every effort to supplement your faith with virtue..." (2 Pt. 1:5).*

During dinner with friends, the husband began to tell a story—nothing urgent or earth-shattering, just a lighthearted recollection. Before he could finish his first sentence, his wife cut him off to correct a minor detail that did not matter in the slightest. He tried again. This time she stayed quiet but shook her head with such intensity that it was impossible to ignore. As he continued, and we all politely pretended not to notice her disapproval, she escalated—swinging her leg, visibly agitated, her face contorted with silent protest. Then finally, with dramatic exasperation, she interrupted again: "I can-NOT believe you won't admit it was Mazatlán and not—" Cabo? Venezuela? Rocky Point? I honestly don't remember what location she insisted on, because it had zero bearing on the story. What

I do remember is how painfully uncomfortable we felt for him. My husband and I wanted to come to his defense, and I found myself blurting out, "Does it really matter?!"

Emasculation of men has become sport. We see it in almost every scenario – From the movie screen to the live stream. Men are stupid and women save the world. It is very difficult to watch and as we ponder how we got here, we must admit, it has been stirring for quite some time now.

There is nothing new under the sun—it's just more exposed now. What once hid behind closed doors is paraded in plain sight. I see it constantly: women belittling their husbands, often cloaked in humor or disguised as prayer requests. It shows up in women's prayer groups that slowly shift into gripe sessions: "what's wrong with my spouse," or comments like, "We need to pray for Margie… I'm pretty sure her husband is drinking again." Let's be honest—much of this isn't intercession. It. Is. Gossip.

And then there is the entertainment we consume. In sitcoms like *Everybody Loves Raymond*, it's considered funny— even endearing— to call your husband an "idiot."

But here's the truth: that is not humor. It is dishonor. And ladies… it is NOT okay.

We are in the middle of a war against men—a war on masculinity, on headship, and on God's design for marriage. And it must end with us.

"In the beginning, God…" (Gen. 1:1). The Hebrew word used for God here is *Elohim*—a grammatically singular, masculine noun with a plural ending. *El* (masculine singular for "God") + *-ohim* (a plural suffix in

Hebrew) = *Elohim* — a single, masculine God expressed in a plural form. It is a linguistic echo of the Trinity right from the very first verse.

It's one of the Bible's first and clearest mysteries: God is one (Deut. 6:4), yet His very name in the creation account declares the Trinity. He is not many Gods, but rather One <u>masculine</u> God in three persons, a truth more fully revealed in the New Testament (John 1:1–3; Matt. 28:19).

When we contend for biblical masculinity and headship, we are not championing cultural tradition—we are standing for the very nature of the God we serve, who has revealed Himself in masculine terms and designed men to reflect His image in leadership, provision, and strength. Our husbands were created by Him, through Him, and for Him (Col. 1:16; John 1:3). To fight for your husband's right to be a man—to lead, to protect, to bear responsibility—is to fight for the honor of God's design and ultimately, for God's right to be God.

"Death and life are in the power of the tongue" (Pr. 18:21). When we tear down our husbands with our words, we are not just mocking them— we are mocking the role God assigned them. "Let the wife see that she respects her husband" (Eph. 5:33). That's not a cultural suggestion; that is a biblical command.

Christian women must rise up and say, "No more." Standing up for our husbands is not just defending a man—it's defending marriage. It is defending God's design. It is declaring to a watching world that we believe in His principles, His Word, and His wisdom. When we honor our husbands, we are ultimately honoring the Lord.

*"For the weapons of our warfare are not of the flesh but have divine power to destroy strongholds" (2 Cor. 10:4).*

This is spiritual warfare—and it begins in our hearts, our homes, and our words.

Christ's relationship with His bride is demonstrated in the holy bonds of our marriage.

There are two foundational elements in every relationship: security and significance. While closely connected, we'll begin with security—the bedrock of trust and emotional safety. The day after our uncomfortable dinner, the woman who had publicly belittled her husband called me. She shared that her husband had declared he would never go out in public with her again. Internally, I thought, well, that makes three of us! My husband and I had come to the same conclusion. If even we, as mere observers, felt unsafe in her presence, how much more must he?

How could he possibly feel secure in that relationship? Security is a God-woven need in both men and women. Every person longs to feel safe—emotionally, relationally, even spiritually. We need to know that the one we love will not wound us, mock us, or expose us to shame. Scripture commands, "Love one another with brotherly affection. Outdo one another in showing honor" (Rom. 12:10). That applies especially in marriage.

Providing your spouse with the unshakable assurance that you will never cause him harm—physically, emotionally, or verbally—is not just kindness; it is a holy virtue, a reflection of Christ's love for the Church.

It is life changing.

A secure spouse is a flourishing spouse. And a home built on security becomes a refuge, not a battlefield.

Scripture paints a high and holy view of womanhood. The Bible says that a wise man's house contains precious treasure (Pr. 21:20)—and that treasure, in context, includes a godly wife. We are called a "good thing" (Pr. 18:22), and when a man finds a wife, he finds favor from the Lord. We are to be women of virtue, who "do our husbands good and not harm, all the days of [our] lives" (Pr. 31:12).

That is God's standard.

But when a man is constantly criticized, rejected, and dishonored, his soul begins to retreat. Human nature seeks relief from unrelenting pain. When Scripture addresses the bitter, quarrelsome woman, God does not ask what her husband did to provoke her. He simply says: "It is better to live in a desert land than with a quarrelsome and fretful woman" (Pr. 21:19) and again, "Better to live on the corner of a roof than in a house shared with a contentious wife" (Pr. 25:24). That is sobering.

When respect is withdrawn and replaced with sarcasm, control, or contempt, a wife may unknowingly slip into the "captain's chair"—steering the household with unspoken dominance. Her voice may quiet, but her presence becomes heavy—not heard but felt. A slow, heavy sadness begins to settle over the home. And over time, she drives the ship of her family straight into the ground—or worse, capsizes it. And when that happens, there may be no survivors.

We, as women, hold more power than we often realize. Through our words, our tone, our silence, even our body language, we are either building a sanctuary or excavating a grave. I have seen this more apparent in the South – bless their cold, black hearts.

We have pretentiousness on one side of the spectrum: sweet tea pretenders – polished, polite, and not-so-quietly condescending on the other. On the other hand, the mousey silent, Stepford Wives – all smiles with no substance, dying inside, but never daring to say a word, lay right smack-dab in the middle.

None are examples of biblical womanhood. God didn't call us to fake nice, and He didn't call us to fade into the wallpaper. He called us to be wise, kind, strong, gentle, and brave — all under the Lordship of Christ.

That kind of virtue isn't a personality type. It is Spirit-formed character.

In both cases, we have women who would never speak to a friend in the way they speak to their husbands or children. But when we do it in our homes, the damage is deeper—because the wounds cut at the very place that was meant to be safe.

A man can be run so far into emotional depletion that he seeks refuge wherever he can find it.

Sometimes it is in his work—he exhausts himself to avoid the pain at home. Sometimes, tragically, it is in the arms of someone else. And it almost always begins with someone who was "just a friend."

**Virtue in the Face of a Fool: Abigail's Example**

Scripture gives us a living example of this kind of virtue in the life of **Abigail.**

Abigail was married to a foolish, harsh, and drunken man (1 Samuel 25:3). Scripture does not excuse his behavior, soften it, or spiritualize it away. Nabal was sinful, reckless, and arrogant—and Abigail knew it.

Yet when Nabal's actions placed their household in mortal danger, Abigail did not respond with panic, rebellion, or public shaming. She acted with wisdom.

When she approached David—then a young, soon-to-be king—she did not insult her husband, exaggerate his failures, or emotionally unload. She stated the facts plainly, took responsibility for intervention, and appealed to righteousness, justice, and God's purposes (1 Samuel 25:24–31).

Abigail modeled strength under control. She neither defended sin nor used it as justification for disrespect. She acted decisively, spoke truthfully, and trusted God with the outcome.

God dealt with Nabal Himself. His death was sudden and unmistakable (1 Samuel 25:38). And in time, God reminded David of Abigail's wisdom and virtue—and she became his wife (1 Samuel 25:39–42).

This is not a promise that every difficult marriage ends the same way— but it *is* a clear reminder: God sees. God judges rightly. And God honors women who act with wisdom, restraint, and faith rather than reaction, rebellion, or revenge.

While writing this book, I asked my husband many questions—I wanted a man's perspective, unfiltered and honest. One of the things David shared stood out with crystal clarity. He said that during his years of dating, one of the most disheartening trends he noticed was the lasting damage the feminist movement had inflicted on many women. What once may have started as a fight for value and dignity had, in many cases, morphed into an attitude of hardness and isolation.

David put it simply: One of the most unattractive qualities he encountered in today's so-called "modern woman" was the bold assertion: 'I don't need a man.' He said, "Men _want_ to be needed. We _desire_ to feel needed" *(emphasis, his)*.

That longing to be needed isn't about ego—it's about design. God created man with a heart to lead, protect, and provide. From the beginning, God said, "It is not good that the man should be alone; I will make him a helper fit for him" (Genesis 2:18). To tell a man, "I don't need you," is to reject the very role God ordained—and, by extension, to reject a portion of His divine image.

This isn't about becoming dependent or weak. It's about understanding that interdependence within marriage reflects the very heart of God's design. Men and women were never intended to compete for headship— but to complement one another in mutual honor and covenantal purpose.

When a woman says, "I need you—not because I'm lacking, but because we are better together"—that speaks life into a man's soul. It builds his confidence, affirms his role, and honors his Maker.

*"The voice of my beloved! Behold, he comes, leaping over the mountains, bounding over the hills. My beloved is like a gazelle or a young stag. Behold there he stands... My beloved speaks and says to*

Find your Scripture that speaks to you about your beloved. And then girl—WRITE THEM DOWN! Stick them to the fridge. Tape them to the mirror (dry erase markers work too). Make a sticker for your coffee mug if you must! Better yet— text him! Drop a verse from Song of Solomon, "Your arms are rods of gold, set with jewels" and although you may never see it, just know you have made him smile.

Because listen: men need to hear that you love them. That you <u>need</u> them. You <u>desire</u> them. The world needs to *see* that you love them. Your beloved needs to see it, feel it, maybe even taste it (yes, I'm talking about the cookies and the kisses). Even if the only thing your husband did today was make it home in one piece and remember where you live— celebrate it! Open that door like you've just won the love lottery and kiss that man right on the mouth!

Yes, ma'am. No holy peck on the cheek. No pat on the back like he's your uncle at Thanksgiving. Kiss. That. Man. With joy, on purpose, and with a little praise to Jesus for keeping him safe.

# ✦ DEVOTIONAL — VIRTUE ✦

*Holy but Spicy: The Sanctified Sass of a Virtuous Woman*

◆◆◆

**REFOCUS: Doctrine/Truth**

Your words and actions toward your husband are not just relational—they're spiritual. Virtue begins not with appearance or ability, but with the heart. Proverbs 31:12 says, "She does him good, and not harm, all the days of her life." When we honor our husbands with our mouths, our tone, and our presence, we are displaying our reverence for the Lord (Eph. 5:33). A wife's virtue is not measured by perfection, but by her posture of honor—toward both God and her husband.

**REPRIORITIZE:  Action/Obedience**

1. **Guard the Door of Your Mouth**

    Pr. 21:23 – "Whoever keeps his mouth and his tongue keeps himself out of trouble." Speak words that give life, not wounds. No sarcastic zingers, eyerolls, or public corrections—those are soul killers.

2. **Greet Him Like You're Glad He Exists**

    Proverbs 31:23 says her husband is "known in the gates." Let him be known in your community as a man who is cherished, honored and deserving of honor. Respected and deserving of respect.

    Meet him at the door. Kiss him intentionally.

Let him feel your joy that he is home.

3.  **Say the Good Stuff Out Loud – And in the Streets**

    Philippians 4:8 – "Think about these things…" and then say them. Send a text. Leave a note. Post a Song of Solomon verse on his Facebook page. Yes, really.

4.  **Let Your Strength Be Tender**

    Proverbs 31:26 – "She opens her mouth with wisdom, and the teaching of kindness is on her tongue."

Strong women build peaceful homes—not by volume or dominance, but by wisdom, gentleness, and grace.

## THE BOTTOM LINE:

Virtue is visible. It shows up in your voice, your words, your tone, your touch. When we act with honor toward our husbands, we're not just being "good wives"—we're being faithful disciples of Christ. The virtuous woman's home isn't perfect, but it is filled with life, laughter, and love that reflects her Redeemer. And it begins with her.

## REFLECT: Journal Prompts

- When do I struggle most to honor my husband in my words or attitude?

- How can I express appreciation to him this week—out loud and on purpose?

- Have I unknowingly used sarcasm or silence to hurt? How can I change that?

- What verse can I memorize to remind me to build, not break?

## RESPOND: Prayer

*Before I ask You for strength, I confess where I have reacted in the flesh instead of walking in wisdom, restraint, and trust in You.*

*Lord, make my heart soft, my words wise, and my presence peaceful. Let my mouth be a fountain of kindness, not criticism. Teach me to cherish my husband, not control him. Help me reflect You—faithfully, joyfully, and with honor. Let virtue start in my thoughts and overflow into my words, for Your glory and the good of my home. Amen.*

*"Men ought not to content themselves with a general repentance, but it is every man's duty to endeavor to repent of his particular sins, particularly." (See Westminster Confession 15.5).*

Repentance is a daily act of worship, faith, and obedience.

# Knowledge

## Theology Is not Just for Bearded Men in Basements

*"The lips of knowledge are a precious jewel" (Pr. 20:15).*

Knowledge is power! So, the old saying goes… and rightfully so does the Bible. A woman without knowledge does not have wisdom and without knowledge her virtue will not have the additional building blocks required to build her home. Here is what the Bible says about those who seek after knowledge and the benefits of that acquisition:

- They are wise (Prov. 18:15).
- Wise = Knowledge (Prov. 8:12).
- They are intelligent (Prov. 15:14).
- Storing knowledge is wise. (Prov. 10:14).
- Knowledge & wisdom tame your tongue (15:2).
- Their lips spread more knowledge (Prov. 15:7).
- They are prudent (Prov. 13:16).
- They are disciplined (Prov. 12:1).
- They are in the advantage (Ecc. 7:12).
- They are discerning (Hos. 14:9).

- They are increasing in power (Prov. 24:5)

- They are delivered (Prov. 11:9)

- Their rooms are filled with riches (Prov. 24:4).

- Their soul is at peace (Prov. 2:10).

- They are just (Mic. 3:1).

- They know the truth and are free (Jn. 8:32).

- They are blessed (John 13:17)

- They are enriched (1 Cor. 1:5).

- God wants all men to come to a knowledge of the truth (1 Tim 2:4).

The Holy Spirit's power is what controls our tongue and keeps our thoughts pure… When we don't over run it with ourselves, that is: "The thief comes to kill and destroy…" (Jn. 10:10).

It really stinks when we are our own thief.

The Bible explains that there is an order however – To get knowledge and understanding we must first seek out God himself – That is theology. Women need theology. I cannot stress that enough!

In a sermon, one of the greatest preachers of our day, Paul Washer, nailed it:

> My wife doesn't need to go to one of those silly women's conferences that's titled, 'If the world gives you lemons, learn how to make lemonade.' My wife needs theology, because she's

a believer, and women grown in grace the same way men do. Through the study of Scripture.[14]

Theology is the study of God and His nature. If you do not have theology – You do not know Who God is. Without theology, you will never know doctrine. That is, what God <u>expects</u> from you: God's law, principals, ethics, values, etc.

We musts learn to respect Him (fear of the Lord) for who He is – (Theology) and that is the thrice Holy, Great, I Am, who was and is and is to come, worthy of honor, glory, and blessing (Rev. 12:1,Ex 3:14, Rev 1:8, 5:12, ); in order to know our purpose in His plan (Doctrine) to glorify Him in everything we are and everything we do (1 Cor. 10:31).

*"If you seek it like silver and search for it as for hidden treasures, then you will understand the fear of the Lord and find the knowledge of God. For the Lord gives wisdom; from his mouth come knowledge and understanding" (Proverbs 2:4-6).*

The Bible refers to that as having a "fear" of God. It simply means having an awe and reverence. Without a reverence for our Holy Father, we cannot be the woman He has designed us to be. We must seek a deeper relationship with our Lord in order to deepen our relationship with our husbands. To know God is the first step in getting to know His plans for you and your role as your husband's helper.

---

[14] *The video link for this sermon has been removed from the internet due to G3 copyright (and their mandate to have a paid subscription to listen to the gospel be preached). However, that's where he preached the sermon (at a G3 conference) and where we first heard it.*

We must be searching diligently – as if we were mining for a precious metal like gold or silver or searching for hidden treasure that is worth more than our imagination – and that treasure is wisdom. So – the order is this: To get knowledge and understanding, you must obtain wisdom, which comes by the "fear of the Lord" which can only be obtained by persistently studying and believing by faith in the Holy Word of our Living God – *"if you seek it like silver and search for it as for hidden treasures, then you will understand the fear of the Lord and find the knowledge of God. For the Lord gives wisdom; from his mouth come knowledge and understanding"* (Prov. 2:4-6).

"Everyone's a theologian. The question is: is your theology sound?" – R. C. Sproul

## CLEANING HOUSE: FRIENDSHIPS, COUNSEL & THE GODLY GIRL GLOW-UP

Let's talk about something crucial but not-so-comfy: Your circle.

Yes — we need Godly counsel, and not just from podcasts or Reels. We need real-life, like-minded, Scripture-soaked, theologically sound women in our lives. Not just "Christian-ish" but legit disciples who know the difference between Ephesians and Etsy.

*"Do not be unequally yoked with unbelievers. For what partnership has righteousness with lawlessness? Or what fellowship has light with darkness?" (2 Cor. 6:14)* — *yes, 2nd Corinthians, not 1st, your coffee mug lied.*

Let's be honest: some of the "friends" we've kept around are not on this journey with us.

Some are more interested in brunch gossip than biblical growth. And when you start getting serious about Jesus — like, for real — you will shine some light into dark places.

I've been there.

I had to let go of a whole crew of women who weren't helping me grow in Christ — in fact, they were holding me back like spiritual ankle weights. I prayed, quietly stepped back from toxic conversations, and politely exited the "girls' night" routines that had zero edification and a whole lot of chaos.

I started blogging about marriage and biblical relationships, and guess what? One by one, they dipped out. Blinded by the light.

I didn't slam any doors. I just turned on the lights. And when that happens? Let's just say... you find out how many cockroaches were living rent-free in your spiritual house. They scatter.

Let them.

God will provide what you lose for the sake of His name — real friends, deeper community, greater joy. (Luke 18:29–30, anyone?)

So now what?

You're standing in a clean house... maybe a little echoey. No friends, your husband thinks you've joined a cult, and you're bouncing around the house singing worship songs with dinner ready, laundry folded, kids thriving — and you're not in pajamas when he gets home?

But you're not naked yet?

Huh. That's okay — we're working on sanctification in stages.

But listen this is all normal when you follow Christ against the grain of the world.

## THIS WORLD IS NOT YOUR FRIEND

Let's be clear: we live in a world that is 100% against biblical womanhood — and it shows.

We're told never to be content — always hustle, grind, climb, chase.

Women are now the center of every commercial, every show, every storyline.

The cultural script is loud and clear:

Men are clueless. Women are queens. Men mess everything up. Women fix it all.

And somehow, we're supposed to call this "progress."

Let's be real: it's not empowerment — it's emasculation.

This kind of narrative strips men of their God-given role – treats fathers like idiots, husbands like children, and manhood like a threat.

It trains us — subtly, constantly — to expect nothing from men except failure and passivity. And then we wonder why men disengage, why marriages collapse, why homes feel unstable.

Here's the truth: When men are dishonored, families unravel.

God created men to lead with strength, humility, sacrifice, and conviction — not to be sidelined, mocked, or ignored.

And no, biblical manhood isn't toxic. Sin is toxic.

What culture calls "toxic masculinity" is often just corrupted leadership — and you don't fix that by erasing men. You fix it by redeeming them in Christ.

This isn't just bad storytelling — it's spiritual sabotage.

Because when you emasculate men, you disrupt God's created order. And when you disrupt that? You don't just lose headship — you lose protection, provision, vision, and peace.

We need strong men — not perfect men, but biblically grounded, Spirit-led, truth-speaking men.

And we need women who honor that, not compete with it.

If you're single — there's an app (or twelve).

Swipe, scroll, flirt, ghost, repeat.

If you're married — there's a lawyer on standby, or worse, an entire affair service (yes, Ashley Madison is still out here ruining souls).

If you want expensive clothes you can't afford — just finance your insecurity with a shiny new credit card.

And then we wonder why contentment feels like a fossil.

The world sells discontentment as ambition and covetousness as self-care. It tells us to chase the next thing, trade up, glow up, level up — but never settle down into faithfulness.

Biblical contentment doesn't sell well, because it can't be bought. It's learned through surrender (Phil. 4:11–13), grown through gratitude, and grounded in the truth that God really is enough.

So yes — the culture's chaos makes contentment feel outdated. But in Christ, contentment is a rebellion against the world — and a declaration that He is better.

Then there's the S-word... Submission.

Whew. Just saying, it costs you a group of friends and half your extended family at Thanksgiving.

But what's wild? The submission I'm talking about isn't even toward my husband (yet) — Rather, it is my submission to Christ.

And people still lost their minds.

**THE COST OF OBEDIENCE**

To obey Christ is to trust His Word — what He says about:

- Christ Himself
- Me
- My purpose
- This broken world
- My marriage
- My kids
- My family
- My calling

And what did that obedience cost me?

Friends? Reputation? Comfort?

Yeah. All of the above.

But was it worth it?

Let me say it plain:

Absolutely. 100%. Without a doubt. Worth it.

Because He is worth it.

My dear girlfriend — let me tell you something: You are on the brink of discovering a kind of freedom that is mind-blowing, thrilling, soul-tingling, and peace-soaked.

It's electrifying and serene. It's fierce and still.

It is nothing short of above and beyond all that you could ever ask, think, or imagine (Eph. 3:20).

And the best part?

It doesn't come from getting everything you want — it comes from surrendering to the One who already gave you everything you need.

*For this reason I bow my knees before the Father, from whom every family in heaven and on earth is named, that according to the riches of his glory he may grant you to be strengthened with power through his Spirit in your inner being, so that Christ may dwell in your hearts through faith—that you, being rooted and grounded in love, may have strength to comprehend with all the saints what is the breadth and length and height and depth, and to know the love of Christ that surpasses knowledge, that you may be filled with all the fullness of God (Eph. 3:14-19).*

## *Theology Is not Just for Bearded Men in Basements*

◆◆◆

### REFOCUS: Doctrine/Truth

- Knowledge isn't just about cramming facts or sounding smart in a Bible study — it's about knowing God (Jer. 9:23–24).

- Real knowledge transforms you from the inside out. It guards your mind, tames your tongue, fuels your discernment, and brings actual peace to your soul (Prov. 2:10; 15:2).

- If you don't know what God says, you'll believe whatever the world says — and that's how spiritual sinkholes form.

***Truth Bomb:*** *You cannot follow a God you don't know.*

### REPRIORITIZE: Action/Obedience

Here's your practical game plan — no seminary degree required:

- Start your day with Scripture before social media. Even if it's just one chapter. One verse. One thought. Start there.

- Ask questions. Don't just read. Study. What does this passage say about God? About me? About the gospel? Who wrote this? When was it written? What was the culture in that day? How does this point back to the Cross? (because it always does!)

*Side Note: I do not always have time for a study session with my Bible. So, I keep a journal specific to the particular book that I am ready and jot down my notes. Then, I can set aside time each week, where I truly study (connect the dots of OT and NT truths). I do not go on to another book until I have thoroughly examined each sentence of the first one. Hermeneutics needs to become a part of your theological vocabulary. We do not have time to talk about it here in this book, but I urge you: Look it up. Learn it. Then Study hard!*

- Pick up a solid commentary. (Matthew Henry. John MacArthur. R.C. Sproul. Yes, even women can read the big books.)

- Talk about what you're learning. Share truth. Discuss it with your kids, your friends, your husband — anyone who'll listen.

- Be teachable. Ask God for humility to grow. Proverbs 12:1 puts it bluntly: Don't be stupid. "Whoever loves discipline loves knowledge, but <u>he who hates reproof is stupid</u>." (Yep. That's in the Bible.)

**THE BOTTOM LINE:**

You were made to know God deeply — not just feel things about Him.

Feelings fade. Truth holds.

The more you know Him, the more you'll love Him.

And the more you love Him, the more your life will look like His.

**REFLECT: Journal Prompts**

- What lies have I believed because I wasn't grounded in Scripture?

- Do I crave spiritual knowledge the way I crave entertainment or affirmation?

- What's stopping me from diving deeper into the Word — and what needs to change?

- How would my relationships change if I spoke from a place of biblical knowledge?

**RESPOND: Prayer Prompts**

Father, before I ask You to move, I confess where I have resisted Your will in ________.

Praise God as the source of all true wisdom and knowledge (Prov. 2:6).

Ask the Spirit to cultivate discernment, humility, and a hunger for truth.

Struggling with doubt or feeling overwhelmed? Ask God for clarity and courage — and remind your heart that even the smallest step toward Him is never wasted.

"What is the chief end of man? To glorify God and enjoy Him forever." You can't glorify a God you don't know. *(See Westminster Shorter Catechism Q. 1.)*.

# Self-Control

## The Forgotten Superpower

*A woman who builds her house and tears it down with her own hands is...*

Have you ever notice that when you begin a new diet that you are a raving lunatic, out of control by lunch time, trying to justify breaking into the vending machine at work, to get your candy-fix for the day... even though you haven't thought about a candy bar in ten years... ? But when we don't think about dieting – (and we are balanced) – we can drop weight without thinking about it.

Okay, so maybe that happened more in your youth than it does now...

That is exactly how it is with our marriages – We become so complacent and so lethargic that we don't even realize that our marriage has lost weight and we are starving it to death.

Let's just go ahead and admit it: self-control is not sexy.

It doesn't get likes on Instagram. It doesn't sell books. And it definitely doesn't get applauded at girls' night.

But it should.

Because self-control is the quiet force that holds biblical womanhood together. It's the gatekeeper of godly words, wise choices, holy desires, disciplined habits, and yes — spicy, spirit-filled marriages.

Self-control is not about gritting your teeth and muscling through temptation. It's not about willpower, perfection, or keeping your house looking like a Pinterest board. It is an attribute of the fruit of the Spirit (Gal. 5:22–23).

It is evidence that Christ is alive in you and that the Holy Spirit is doing business in your heart.

Titus 2? That cornerstone passage on biblical womanhood? It repeats one thing like a drumbeat: <u>Self-control</u>.

*Older women should be reverent... not slanderers... they are to teach what is good... and to train the younger women to be self-controlled... (Titus 2:3–5)*

And why does Paul say all this? "So that the word of God may not be reviled." In other words: your lack of self-control can discredit the gospel you claim to believe.

> *"If you can't say Amen, you ought to say Ouch!" -Voddie Baucham*

This isn't just about donuts and drive-thru budgets (although yes, that too). Self-control shows up when:

You don't respond to your husband's tone with a sharper one of your own.

You pause before hitting "send" on that flaming-hot group text reply.

You choose Scripture over scrolling when your heart is heavy or your morning is rushed.

You hold your tongue instead of giving that "bless her heart" commentary.

You stay quiet, not because you're weak, but because the Holy Spirit is strong in you.

*"A man without self-control is like a city broken into and left without walls" (Pr. 25:28).*

Translation: without self-control, you are spiritually exposed. Emotionally vulnerable. Wide open to offense, manipulation, distraction, and burnout.

Let's be real — self-control is hard. It's slow. It requires restraint in a world that rewards indulgence. The culture says: "If it feels good, do it." The Spirit says: "Walk by the Spirit, and you will not gratify the desires of the flesh." (Gal. 5:16)

You can't have both. One will rule. One will wither.

Every woman has her battleground. Maybe it's food. Or spending. Or flirting. Or sarcasm. Or comparison. Or control. Or social media. Or impulse shopping on Amazon Prime at 11:47 PM.

But behind all of those is one root question:

Who's in charge — the flesh, or the Spirit? Self-control isn't just about what you say no to. It's about what you can now say YES to:

- Peace in your home
- Freedom from regret

- Trust in your marriage

- Respect from your kids

- A clean conscience before the Lord

- Joy in obedience — the real kind

Self-control is not just about saying no to sin — it's about saying yes to everything God says is good.

And it shows up in all kinds of places we don't always connect to discipline:

1. **In the Word** — "She opens her mouth with wisdom..." (Pr. 31:26)

   You can't speak truth if you don't know truth. Reading the Word isn't optional for the Christian woman — it's oxygen. It takes self-control to shut the laptop, put down the phone, or get up earlier to meet with God. But nothing will transform your tone, your parenting, your marriage, or your mind more than consistently soaking in Scripture.

   Use a Bible. Not an electronic Bible but one that you can underline and make notes in. One that becomes as valuable as your phone – but is not your phone.

2. **In the Home** — "She looks well to the ways of her household..." (Pr. 31:27)

   Homemaking is not drudgery. It's dominion. It takes self-control to tend your home instead of numbing out online. To fold laundry when you'd rather ignore it. To cook… again.

To budget. To scrub that bathroom floor for the third time this week. It is not beneath you. It is entrusted to you.

3.  **In Modesty** — "Strength and dignity are her clothing..." (Pr. 31:25)

    Modesty is not about hiding your body — it's about revealing your reverence. It's the spiritual discipline of dressing in a way that honors God, your husband (or future husband), and the watching world. Modesty takes self-control — to resist trends that scream for attention, to reject the lie that more skin equals more value.

4.  **In Strength and Stewardship** — "She dresses herself with strength and makes her arms strong." (Pr. 31:17)

    This isn't just poetic language — it's intentional. She "makes her arms strong" — because she knows her body is a vessel of worship, work, and witness. This is a woman who takes care of her body. Not out of vanity, but out of stewardship. Not because she's obsessed with her figure, but because she's serious about her faith.

    Your health matters. Your energy matters. Your ability to serve your family, love your neighbor, and run your race — it all connects back to how you treat the temple God gave you (1 Cor. 6:19–20).

Self-control says:

- I will move my body even when I don't feel like it.
- I will fuel myself with what gives life, not what drains it.

- I will rest like I trust God — not overdo it like it all depends on me.

- She is not chasing a bikini body — she is pursuing longevity, vitality, and godly readiness.

5. **In Sacrifice** — "If anyone would come after me, let him deny himself and take up his cross daily..." (Lk. 9:23).
Self-control means dying to self.
Every. Single. Day.

It means picking up the cross when your flesh says, "no thanks." It means showing up in your marriage when you don't feel "in love." It means laying down your right to be right. It means saying "yes, Lord," even when it hurts.

## WHAT'S AT STAKE?

Without self-control, you will:

- Neglect the Word
- Resent your home
- Demand attention
- Idolize comfort
- Harbor bitterness
- Build your kingdom instead of His

But with self-control?

- You become a woman of peace
- A woman of purpose
- A woman who builds instead of breaks (Prov. 14:1)

Biblical womanhood without self-control is just cultural chaos with a verse slapped on top.

But with self-control?

She is fierce, faithful, fruitful, and full of the Holy Spirit.

Self-control doesn't restrict your freedom. It is the pathway to it.

I realize that we are women, we are strong, but we are tired! And if you feel like you've blown it a hundred times already today — take heart. Self-control isn't a personality trait. It's a Spirit-born virtue, which means it does not come from you. It comes from God. And if you're in Christ, you already have access to it. You just need to train it (1 Tim. 4:7) – and this begins with dying to yourself and picking up your cross. And we do this daily, remembering "God's mercies are new each morning."

# ✦ DEVOTIONAL — SELF-CONTROL ✦

*The Forgotten Superpower*

◆◆◆

**REFOCUS: Doctrine/Truth**

Let's be honest: self-control doesn't exactly trend well. It's not flashy. It doesn't get applause. It rarely goes viral. But biblically? It's a fruit of the Spirit (Gal. 5:22–23) and one of the clearest evidences of a woman walking in the Spirit instead of being driven by the flesh.

Self-control is the backbone of biblical womanhood. It shows up in what we say, what we wear, what we watch, what we eat, what we post, how we spend, and yes — even how we respond to our husbands. It's what allows us to act like grown Spirit-led women instead of reacting like toddlers with lip gloss.

Titus 2:3–5 says that older women are to be "self-controlled," and they're supposed to teach younger women to do the same. Which means this isn't optional — it's discipleship.

Why does it matter? Because a woman without self-control is like a city broken into and left without walls (Pr. 25:28). Vulnerable. Defenseless. Exhausted. Wide open to every lie, temptation, and manipulation.

You want peace? Start with self-control.

## REPRIORITIZE: Action/Obedience

Self-control isn't about being perfect. It is about being completely and totally surrendered.

It's not about trying harder. It is about training in righteousness (1 Tim. 4:7).

Here's how to put it into practice:

- Tame your tongue (Prov. 15:1). Don't say everything you feel.

- Check your triggers. What are your impulse zones? Shopping? Social media? Sugar? Silence?

- Preach truth to your emotions. Don't let feelings rule the day. Feelings make a terrible god.

- Pause before you post. That 5-second delay could save your relationship (and your witness).

- Feed the Spirit, not the flesh. What you consume shapes your character.

- Steward your body. Your health is a spiritual issue. Make your arms strong (Pr. 31:17). Move. Rest. Nourish. Not to be admired — but to be able.

- Watch your wallet. Self-control is also financial. Budgeting isn't bondage — it's wisdom. Debt isn't just an inconvenience — it's often the fruit of undisciplined desires.

## THE BOTTOM LINE:

Self-control is not restrictive. It's protective. It guards your joy, your peace, your marriage, your witness, your worship. It's not weakness — it's power under control. That's what Jesus modeled, and what the Spirit empowers in you.

## REFLECT: Journal Prompts

- Where in my life am I most prone to react instead of respond?

- What desires or emotions tend to control me more than I control them?

- Am I stewarding my health with intentionality or neglecting my body in the name of busyness or comfort?

- How does my spending reflect (or contradict) self-control?

- Who is watching me live out (or fail to live out) this attribute of the fruit of the Spirit? *(Children, family, friends, church people, community, your work people)? It's more people than you think, that's for sure!*

## RESPOND: Prayer Prompts

Before I ask You for self-control, I confess where I have indulged comfort, distraction, or entitlement instead of obedience.

Praise God that He is slow to anger, abounding in steadfast love, and perfectly self-controlled in all His ways (Ex. 34:6).

Ask the Holy Spirit to help you cultivate restraint, discipline, and holy habits in body, mind, and resources.

Feel like you've failed too many times to try again? Be honest with God. Ask Him to retrain your heart and renew your will (Rom. 12:2).

What is sanctification? It is the work of God's grace whereby we are more and more enabled to die unto sin and live unto righteousness. *(See Westminster Larger Catechism Q. 75).*

# The Empty Nest (Isn't Empty)

## From Empty Nest to Holy Flame

*Hello. My name is Holly. What was your name again?*

This isn't a chapter about home décor. This is about soul restoration. The empty nest is not the end of the story; it's a new beginning for rediscovering your husband, reigniting intimacy, and reframing your identity in Christ. Put down the Pinterest board. Stop looking for identity in church projects. You were already given a calling: To be his wife. To be his crown. To be his beautiful.

Let this chapter be your re-entry into passion—both spiritual and physical.

**So… the kids are gone.**

You have cried. You have sorted through 4,000 Crayola masterpieces. You have organized the closet, labeled the spice jars, and—if you're like many of us—turned your daughter's room into a monogrammed haven of crafting dreams, complete with a glue gun altar and a drawer for every shade of glitter vinyl.

You may have even considered buying a goat and grinding your own wheat, because a Christian YouTuber said your soul depends on it.

We joke…

…Kind of.

But here's the point: We are deeply vulnerable here.

Especially Christian women. Especially mothers. Especially those of us who are just now realizing that for nearly two decades, our "ministry" was measured in carpool miles, packed lunches, and bedtime prayers.

And now we're wondering: What now?

**Where the Rubber Meets the Road**

This is not the time to go looking for significance inside hustles, six-figure dreams, or fifteen different ministries at church.

It's time to return to your first ministry: your marriage.

*"Whatever you do, do all to the glory of God" (1 Cor. 10:31).*

Yes, even that includes your love life. Your home life. Your marriage bed.

This isn't the time to run from your husband—it's the time to run toward him.

**The Mirror, the Myth, and the Menopause**

Let's address the elephant in the closet: spandex.

Sure, they feel like they fit. But girl… they lie.

And this is not the time to go back in time and relive the 1950's either.

And no, that's not the "this year's" version of you in the mirror. That's the version that's raised a family, survived PTA meetings, conquered casseroles, and deserves a trophy. Or at least a nap.

But your husband?

He doesn't see flaws. He sees his beloved.

*"You are altogether beautiful, my love; there is no flaw in you."*

*(Song 4:7)*

You are his standard of beauty. You are his joy. You are still his bride.

**You Are Not Just His Wife… You are His Playground**

Paul's warning in 1 Timothy 5:13 (busybodies), was not aimed at women by accident. We are, by nature and habit, expert busybodies—masters of motion, chatter, and mental checklists. The danger is that those same checklists don't always stop at the kitchen door; they follow us straight into the bedroom.

Somewhere between responsibility and restlessness, we forget how to surrender. We say we want rest, but what we really want is control—with our feet up.

My husband once tried to help me with this. He drew me a bath. Candles. Music. Cocktail. The whole spa-day-at-home situation. It was thoughtful. Intentional. Sweet.

I lasted about five minutes.

The water was too hot. The "relaxing rainforest" soundtrack apparently featured birds being actively murdered. My hands were wet, so I couldn't wipe my sweating face. My hair was frizzing. *Fantastic.* Now there's going to be a ring in the tub—which I *just* cleaned. What am I even soaking in? Now I'm going to have to shower. I don't want to get my hair wet. Where is that stupid dry towel? Why am I sweating in a bath? This defeats the entire purpose of bathing.

By minute three, my inner dialogue sounded less like rest and more like a hostage negotiation.

I finally climbed out once I felt I had stayed in long enough to acknowledge my husband's effort. Was I relaxed? No. But I had successfully proven that even in a perfectly prepared moment of rest, I could still find fifteen problems and solve none of them.

Mission accomplished.

That same inability to slow down shows up in intimacy. When we drag our mental to-do lists into the bedroom, surrender is replaced with efficiency, and what God designed as a place of rest, trust, and yielding becomes just another item to check off—often reduced to a rushed, self-focused moment that lasts only minutes. Biblical submission, even in intimacy, requires something far more difficult for busy women: stillness, trust, and the willingness to let go.

So, before you turn the old nursery into a quilting room, maybe you need to ask:

Have I become his roommate instead of his reward?

Have I stopped being playful because I thought this season was about rest instead of romance?

Have I traded passion for practicality?

Sister, there's still fire in your soul—and it belongs in your marriage bed, not your hobby closet.

*"Let your fountain be blessed and rejoice in the wife of your youth… be intoxicated always in her love." (Pr. 5:18–19)*

## False Significance Is a Trap

This isn't about guilt. It's about glory.

We chase ministry roles, women's retreats, and theology classes (all good things!)—but sometimes, we use them to hide from a marriage we've stopped watering.

**Don't use the church as an excuse to ignore your home.**

*"The heart of her husband trusts in her, and he will have no lack of gain." (Pr. 31:11).*

That trust wasn't built on potlucks and pews. It is built in private. In prayer. In pursuit.

*From Empty Nest to Holy Flame*

**REFOCUS: Doctrine/Truth**

So here's the plan:

Don't go to the playground—be the playground.

Don't live like a widow when your husband's waiting for you on the couch.

Don't become a stranger to the man you vowed your life to.

Instead, take this time to laugh again. To kiss again. To rediscover what you both like. To plan something fun. To let the bedroom become the new "craft room."

This isn't the beginning of the end. It's the beginning of a new glory.

**REPRIORITIZE: Action/Obedience**

**Re-engage Intimately**:

Send him playful texts during the day. Declare "Naked Tuesdays" and follow through. Surprise him with a bath, a shoulder massage, or—like I once did—wait for him on the (enclosed) patio wearing nothing but a smile, with wine, cheese, and crackers. Be bold. Be kind. Be his joy.

**Reconnect Emotionally:**

Ask about his dreams. Laugh together. Watch his favorite movie—even if it's the 400th time you have seen *Gladiator*.

**Redirect Energy:**

Before you launch a new ministry or business, ask: Have I ministered to him today? Make his lunch. Pray over his workday. Leave a note in his sock drawer.

**Reframe Beauty:**

Toss the catalog. Remember what he sees. Let your husband's affection—not culture—shape your confidence.

**Repent Where Needed:**

If you've withheld your affection or prioritized everything else above him, confess it. God's grace meets you here—not to shame you, but to reignite you.

## THE BOTTOM LINE:

You are still the woman he chose. And God has not retired your calling. The empty nest is not empty— it's a holy place, ready to be filled again with passion, purpose, and praise. Don't just repurpose the kids' room. Rekindle your marriage. Reignite your desire. Reclaim your role as his beloved. And rejoice in the new season God has beautifully prepared for you both.

**REFLECT: Journal Prompts**

- In what ways have I found false significance outside the home since my children left?

- What part of myself have I withheld from my husband that I now feel ready to rediscover?

- How can I practically show my husband that I still desire him this week?

- Have I been replacing marital intimacy with busyness, hobbies, or even church work?

- What Scripture can I meditate on to renew my vision of biblical womanhood in this season?

**RESPOND: Prayer:**

*Father, before I ask You to move, I confess where I have resisted Your will in _________. You are the God who sees (Gen. 16:13), the Creator who formed me wonderfully and purposefully (Ps. 139:14), and the Covenant Keeper who makes all things new – even in the late seasons (Isa. 43:19; Rev. 21:5). Lord, plant in me a heart of gentle strength (1 Pet. 3:4), faithful love (Pr. 31:11-12), and joyful intimacy (Song 7:10). Restore what I've withheld, renew what has faded, and revive the joy of loving well. When I feel invisible, unattractive, or ashamed of what age has changed, remind me: The heart is deceitful above all things (Jer. 17:9), and I am called to rise above my feelings and believe in you and in your truth: "My beloved is mine and I am his" (Song 2:16). You do not see with human eyes (1 Sam. 16:7) – and apparently neither does my beloved – so help me believe what you (and he) declare over me. Lord, stir my husband's heart. Draw him to me again – not out of duty, but delight. Give him eyes to see your design in me. Let him lead with tenderness (Cor. 3:19), respond with joy (Pr. 5:18), and pursue our oneness with hope and strength (Eph. 5:25-33).*

# In Sickness and in Health

## Restoring the Years the Locust Has Eaten

*All While They're Chomping Away at my body, my health, and...*

*where did my eyebrows go?*

There he sat. Bodybuilder/ex-football star with his bleached-blond, mullet. Piercing blue eyes. Mustache. Cut-off, mesh, half-shirt. Sitt'n there all hot and sexy after a three-man game of volleyball… and there I was, recent beauty queen winner, itty-bitty young thing… But I blew it. After three years of dating, I left him at the altar. But, when God crossed our path 25 years later, well frankly, not much had changed.

I was still a little, wrinkle-free, size two, he was still a hot, hard-core body builder/fitness trainer. But not even three months into our re-kindled romance – and after meeting with pastors and parents and determining we had wasted enough of God's time – we made our plans to be married… and then, out of nowhere, it hit.

Well, it hit me, anyway.

Perimenopause. It all started at a home party with a bunch of my girlfriends (most of whom were nurses) and I was complaining about being so, desperately, hot.

They laughed.

I had a meltdown - literally… I was melting!

I also realized that at that same time, I was having another issue with a loose back molar and headed to the dentist to find that I had lost over 40% of my bone mass.

I didn't realize until later that men like for you to have all your teeth:

*Your teeth are like a flock of shorn ewes that have come up from the washing, all of which <u>bear twins, and not one among them has lost its young</u>" (Song 4:2)*

I was losing my big-fluffy eighties' hair and my sinuses were wreaking so much havoc that I started taking prednisone just to breathe through the night and obtain some much-needed sleep.

*Side Note: Get a second opinion on those treatment options. I wish I had.*

The next thing I knew, I went from a size two to a size 12 in eight short months!

But, besides getting a false bill of sale – He married me anyway.

Little did he know it was only the beginning…

**The Vow We Meant**

We said, "in sickness and in health."

But what we meant was, "in sickness that comes with quick recovery, minimal side effects, and doesn't mess up date night."

Let's be honest. None of us expected the real weight of those words when we were 25, standing in a white dress and heels that didn't cause our back to ache for three days and caused us to consider buying a knee brace.

But now? Our knees and back are in a permanent state of ache, our hormones are confused – if they have even stuck around at all, and the body we gave to our husband in our youth has changed—sometimes drastically – and the worst part is that it seemed to happen overnight!

And we wonder: Is this still the same marriage? Is this still the same me?

Yes. And no. And God is in both.

**Holy... Wasn't How I Felt (But Hilarious? Yes)**

Hot flashes and night sweats. Hairbrush filling up while most of our hair is falling out—along with our teeth. Eyebrows migrating north for the winter. Libido on permanent sabbatical.

Yeah. Sexy is not a word I would use to describe how I felt on any given day.

This is menopause—God's little cosmic joke that somehow makes you crave dark chocolate, murder, and marriage counseling all in the same hour.

Navigating perimenopause wasn't a graceful spiritual mountaintop—it was a hormonal haunted house.

One minute I'm crying over a puppy food commercial, the next I'm Googling whether prison ministry accepts volunteers with anger management issues.

I went from a rock-hard core to *Where did my core go and who replaced it with pudding?*

One loose tooth exited stage left. A bridge entered like a heroic engineer.

And now that same bridge is gripping another loose molar like it's hanging over a cliff yelling, "DON'T LET GO!"

This is the part of life where nothing is *technically* broken… but everything requires reinforcement.

Muscles that used to show up uninvited now need a written request. Teeth that once stood firm now need teammates.

And gravity? She's been promoted to management.

I bought a dust-buster just to leave it beside the toilet. Why? Because it's just easier to vacuum up all of the hair I've lost, while crying, from a seated position.

Holy? No. Hot? Absolutely—but only in the way that made me consider sleeping on ice packs and installing a fan in my bra. Thank God for doctors who know how to administer epidurals for childbirth—and hormone therapy for everything after it. If ever there was proof that God has a sense of humor, it's that menopause can kill your sex drive while giving your husband more time and testosterone than he knows what to do with.

My bra line was drenched while I stood in worship, trying to hold onto hope as my hormones hijacked my peace.

This is the reality many women never talk about—but need to.

It's where restoration begins.

*"He gives power to the faint, and to him who has no might he increases strength." (Isaiah 40:29)*

Because God doesn't just redeem the dramatic sins—He restores the slow losses, too. The kind that shows up in your mirror, your medicine cabinet, and your marriage.

It's where restoration begins.

**Where Did My Eyebrows Go – or for That Matter – My Butt?**

Sure, dropping a jean size sounds great… until you realize you didn't actually get smaller—your entire butt slid down your legs like a melting candle. Suddenly you have no rear end, but both legs have gained six inches each, like you're auditioning to be a Christian flamingo.

Let's just say the eyebrows packed up and moved out without leaving a forwarding address. One day they were there, quietly doing their job, and the next they were gone—like they were raptured without the rest of my face. So now I try to draw them back on, except no matter how carefully I attempt it, I somehow end up looking permanently shocked. Not surprised… *concerned.* Like I've just witnessed something troubling in the produce aisle and I'm not sure whether to pray or call for assistance.

Meanwhile, the hair that *should* be on my eyebrows has clearly relocated south—sprouting enthusiastically on my chin like it's found its true calling. Gravity giveth, gravity taketh away, and menopause just sits back with a clipboard, checking off boxes like, "Yep… we'll keep that. Move this. Remove those entirely."

Gravity does not care who you are. Neither does menopause. Or autoimmune issues. Or thyroid trouble. Or cancer. Or arthritis. Or that bone-deep fatigue that makes you wonder if naps should be listed as a spiritual discipline.

Sometimes you wake up, look in the mirror, and realize someone borrowed your face, hair, teeth, waistline, energy, and your brain. And, in true Christian fellowship form, they have no plans whatsoever to return what they borrowed.

Somewhere in menopause, our thoughts begin to feel like puzzle pieces someone accidentally hurled into the air. We bend down to gather them—trying to remember what we walked into the room for—and realize our bodies have decided to *streamline operations*.

Efficiency, apparently, is the new goal. Why sneeze *and then* pee when you can do both at once? Why bend over without adding a bonus sound effect? Why separate bodily functions when consolidation saves time?

Menopause is nothing if not economical. Our brains misfire, our bodies multitask without permission, and suddenly stooping, sneezing, laughing, or coughing becomes a high-risk activity requiring advance planning and crossed legs. It's humbling. It's inconvenient. And it's often hilarious—once the embarrassment wears off.

But here's the deeper truth: while our bodies are consolidating functions, our hearts are often fragmenting focus. The mental clutter, the constant self-monitoring, the hyper-awareness of everything that no longer works like it used to—can quietly steal our ability to rest, receive, and surrender. Even intimacy can start to feel like one more thing to manage instead of a place to let go.

Menopause doesn't just rearrange hormones; it exposes how tightly we cling to control—and how desperately we need grace in this season.

…So yes—there I was, staring at the mirror, having a full-blown meeting with myself about gravity, hormones, and the sudden disappearance of both eyebrows and backside. And as much as I wanted to rebuke it, cast it out, or lay hands on it, the reality stood firm:

Some things are simply not coming back this side of glory.

But here's what has not changed:

Your calling as a wife.

Your covenant with your husband.

Your worth in Christ.

> *"So we do not lose heart. Though our outer self is wasting away, our inner self is being renewed day by day." (2 Cor. 4:16).*

You are still being renewed. You are not a has-been. You are a being-made-new. And that means there's still joy, intimacy, laughter, and purpose to be reclaimed—even when the body feels like it's staging a quiet mutiny.

**When Health Feels Like a Stranger**

Chronic illness, injury, or age-related changes can feel like betrayal. You want to serve your husband with energy and affection, but your body has entered its "I don't think so" stage.

This is when vows go from poetry to perseverance.

*"The Lord sustains him on his sickbed; in his illness you restore him to full health" (Ps 41:3).*

Maybe healing is slow. Maybe it never comes in the form you imagined. But restoration is still possible. Laughter again. Romance again. Service again.

Even if it looks different now.

**Strength in a woman doesn't expire. It refines.**

Strength in a godly woman isn't gone just because her metabolism is.

You may feel tired, stretched thin, or betrayed by hormones—but remember, the Bible celebrates women who showed up in their season with grit and holy courage.

Jael wasn't in her twenties when she drove a tent peg through a tyrant's skull. *"Most blessed of women be Jael… she struck Sisera; she crushed his head; she shattered and pierced his temple" (Judges 5:24, 26).*

**Refining the Fire:**

Menopause brings undeniable changes—biologically, emotionally, and relationally. One day you're sleeping like a baby; the next you're awake at 2:37 a.m., negotiating with a ceiling fan and wondering why your internal thermostat has declared mutiny. For many women, this season also ushers in a noticeable decline in sexual desire.

But God's Word offers not only comfort—it offers clarity. Marriage remains a covenant of mutual self-giving, even when desire ebbs, shifts, or needs a nap (1 Cor. 7:3–5).

While a wife's physical drive may diminish, her call to love her husband remains steadfast—not out of compulsion, obligation, or gritted teeth, but as an act of covenantal faithfulness and sacrificial love (Eph. 5:22–33).

This doesn't mean ignoring what your body is doing, pretending nothing has changed, or rebuking your ovaries in the name of Jesus. It means acknowledging reality and responding to it with wisdom, grace, and intentional love.

Scripture invites prayerful creativity, honest communication, and Christlike service—even in intimacy. Sometimes that means affection expressed without a full production, tenderness without the expectation of fireworks, and closeness that says, *"I still choose you,"* even when your hormones have clocked out early.

Joy, in this season, may not always be rooted in arousal—but in covenant loyalty, trust, and a settled love that says, *"My husband's heart safely trusts in me"* (Pr. 31:11–12; 1Pt. 3:1–4).

At the same time, Scripture is equally clear about guarding the heart. We are not free to seek comfort, stimulation, or escape in fantasies, self-gratification, or emotional wandering outside the marriage covenant (Matt. 5:28; Heb. 13:4). We have been warned that looking with lust after another is adultery. That includes having fantasies as well. Don't do it.

Sexual desire is a holy fire—designed for the hearth of marriage, not for private sparks struck in isolation. When we redirect it, even quietly, we don't soothe the fire; we misplace it, and in doing so, we dull our affections rather than heal them – and it will destroy your marriage.

*"Let marriage be held in honor among all, and let the marriage bed be undefiled, for God will judge the sexually immoral and adulterous"*
*(Heb. 13:4).*

And here is the hope: we are not left to muscle through this season in our own strength. The Spirit of God empowers us to walk in purity, renew our minds, and reframe intimacy through truth rather than impulse (Rom. 12:1–2). He teaches us to dwell on what is good, honorable, and lovely—even when our bodies feel anything but cooperative (Phil. 4:8).

Menopause, then, is not the end of intimacy. It is a refining fire—a sanctifying season where covenant love burns deeper, steadier, and more beautifully. Less flash, perhaps. But more warmth. And far more staying power.

*"A wise [wo]man is full of strength; and a [wo]man of knowledge enhances [her] might" (Adapted from Pr. 24:5).*

We don't need youth to have power — We are literally filled with power:

*"That the God of our Lord Jesus Christ, the Father of glory, may give you the Spirit of wisdom and of revelation in the knowledge of him, having the eyes of your hearts enlightened, that you may know what is the hope to which he has called you, what are the riches of his*

*glorious inheritance in the saints, and **what is the immeasurable greatness of his power toward us who believe, according to the working of his great might***" (Eph. 1:17-19, emphasis mine).

Restoration doesn't mean pretending we are 25. It means learning to steward what we have now—with wisdom, humility, and yes… that dreaded word we mentioned earlier:

Discipline.

Somewhere along the journey from newlywed energy to midlife reality, discipline stops feeling like punishment and starts feeling like protection. This is where the older-woman wisdom kicks in. We finally understand that our choices today shape the strength we will or won't have tomorrow. Stewardship isn't glamourous—but it is godly.

So, what does discipline look like in this season?

Eating wisely—not perfectly, but intentionally. This is where we act like grown women who understand that both feast days and fiber matter.

Moving our bodies—not to impress anyone, but to strengthen what God has entrusted to us. Stewardship may look like a walk, a stretch, or a 30-minute workout—not a performance.

Resting without guilt—discipline includes knowing when to stop. Fatigue isn't failure; it's a limit God designed on purpose.

Receiving help without shame—discipline also means admitting we can't do it all and allowing our husbands, our children, (the local cleaning service), or our church family to bless us.

Strength comes from Christ but also His people. He put in your life. It is okay to lean on them. God made this promise to Abraham:

*"And I will make of you a great nation, and I will bless you and make your name great, so that you will be a blessing"* *(Gen 12:2).*

Don't steal their blessing because you have decided that God has dealt you a harsh hand.

In a church of Naomi's, or as she liked to call herself: Mara *(bitter)…*

Be a rebel. Be a Ruth.

You don't have to run a triathlon. You do not have to reclaim a pre-children waistline. You simply have to show up, do what you can with the body you have today, and trust God with the rest.

#  ✦ DEVOTIONAL — IN SICKNESS AND IN HEALTH ✦

*Sovereign Grace, Failing Thermostats, and Covenant Love*

◆◆◆

## REFOCUS: Doctrine/Truth

Your body is not a liability to your marriage; it is the God-given vessel through which love, service, intimacy, and joy are still beautifully possible. Aging does not disqualify you. Hormones do not sideline you. A changing body is not evidence of God stepping back—but of Him shaping you for a new season.

He has not abandoned you to decay. He is restoring what the locusts have eaten—even in the joints that creak, the hormones that revolt, and the laugh lines that tell the story of a woman who has lived, loved, cried, and persevered.

Full restoration may not come until glory—and that is okay. The question is: What will you do with the time He's given you in the meantime? Will it be wise?

This season is not about what is fading; it's about what is deepening.

*"And I am sure of this, that he who began a good work in you will bring it to completion at the day of Jesus Christ" (Phil 1:6).*

**REPRIORITIZE: Action/Obedience**

This season of your life may feel unfamiliar, but it is not unfruitful. Stewardship in midlife is less about recovering what has faded and more about strengthening what remains. Here's how we walk it out with grace—and a little grit:

- Honor your body as a tool of love, not a project to fix.

- Fuel it, move it, rest it, and use it for the glory of God—not for comparison.

- Practice discipline as worship.

- Discipline isn't a diet plan; it's discipleship in action. Every intentional choice is a small rebellion against decay and a quiet "yes" to God.

- Communicate openly with your husband.

- Tell him what you're navigating. Invite him into your needs, your limitations, and your victories. This deepens intimacy—spiritually, emotionally, and yes, physically.

- Release the idol of youthful perfection.

- You are not failing because your eyebrows have relocated. You are human. And God calls humans—not mannequins—to holiness.

- Anchor your identity in Christ, not in collagen.

- Collagen may decrease, but sanctification increases. That's the kind of glow no serum can touch.

**THE BOTTOM LINE:**

Aging is not the enemy. Decay is not defeat. This season—
shifting weight, sagging eyelids, brain fog, and all—is another
place where the love of Christ can shine through your covenant.
You're still in this. And He is still with you.

A Word About Pretentiousness (Sisters… Let's Not.)

Please! Be honest here— this is not the season for
pretentiousness. If God Himself decided to show off His sense
of humor by giving us hot flashes, migrating weight,
disappearing hairlines, and thighs that suddenly think they're
storage units, then surely, we can lighten up too. Aging is not a
moral failure. It is not a spiritual deficiency. It is sanctification
with a laugh track.

We do not have to pretend we're unbothered, unwrinkled, or
unchanged. We do not need to "perform perfection" for social
media, for church, or for our husbands.

Pretending doesn't make us holy; humility does. And sometimes
humility looks like saying, "Yep, everything has shifted south—
but praise God, my joy hasn't."

We can laugh. We should laugh. God wired humor into the
human heart, and He did not revoke that gift once we hit
menopause. If anything, He intensified it—because He knew we
would need it.

- How have I been grieving my changing body more than celebrating God's sustaining grace?

- What lies have I believed about my physical worth in this season? What truths from Scripture correct them?

- In what ways have I pushed my husband away during seasons of sickness, pain, or fatigue?

- What does "restoration" look like in this season? Where is God inviting me to practice discipline – not punishment, but stewardship?

- What truths do I need to believe about my worth, even when I don't feel beautiful?

- What fears do I have about aging? How does the gospel speak directly into those fears?

- Where have I seen God's faithfulness in my body, my health, and my marriage – even in weakness?

As you write in your journal, place each fear beside one of these Scriptures. Let the Word interpret your fears, not your mirror.

### 1. God's Faithfulness Through Aging

*Isaiah 46:4 "Even to your old age I am he, and to gray hairs I will carry you."*

*(However, I did make Dave promise me that he would come dig me up to color mine after I'm gone… yeah, I know, I've still got some  issues).*

**Gospel Truth:** God does not retire His care for you. Aging is not abandonment; it is ongoing covenant faithfulness.

## 2.  The Beauty God Values

*1 Peter 3:3–4 "Do not let your adorning be external… but let your adorning be the hidden person of the heart with the imperishable beauty of a gentle and quiet spirit."*

**Gospel Truth:** What the world calls "aging," God calls imperishable beauty. The beauty that increases—not decreases—with time.

## 3.  The Renewed Inner Life

*2 Corinthians 4:16 "Though our outer self is wasting away, our inner self is being renewed day by day."*

**Gospel Truth**: The gospel promises a daily inward renewal that outpaces outward decline. You are becoming more alive, not less.

## 4.  God's Presence in the Fear of Change

*Psalm 34:4 "I sought the Lord, and he answered me and delivered me from all my fears."*

> *1Peter 3:6 "as Sarah obeyed Abraham, calling him lord. And you are her children, if you do good and do not fear anything that is frightening."*

**Gospel Truth:** Aging brings new fears, but God brings new deliverance. Every fear is met by His nearness and His power.

5. **Strength That Matures, Not Shrinks**

*Psalm 92:14 "They still bear fruit in old age; they are ever full of sap and green."*

**Gospel Truth:** Aging in Christ is not diminishing—it's flourishing. Fruitfulness continues, ripens, and sweetens.

6. **God's Unchanging Love**

*Jeremiah 31:3 "I have loved you with an everlasting love."*

**Gospel Truth**: God's love is not tied to your youth, your body, or your energy. It is everlasting. Eternal. Unmoved.

7. **Eternal Security Over Temporary Decline**

*John 10:28 "I give them eternal life, and they will never perish, and no one will snatch them out of my hand."*

**Gospel Truth:** The gospel reframes aging completely—your soul is secure, your future is fixed, your body is headed toward resurrection.

8. **Wisdom as a Crown**

*Proverbs 16:31 "Gray hair is a crown of glory; it is gained in a righteous life."*

**Gospel Truth:** Aging is not shameful to God—it's honorable. A crown, not a curse.

# RESPOND: Prayer

*Father, before I ask You to move, I confess where I have resisted Your will in _________. You are the Maker of my body and the Keeper of my soul. Thank You that You do not discard me when my strength fades or when my body changes. Teach me to steward this season with humility, discipline, and joy. Help me love my husband well—with the energy I have, the wisdom I have gained, and the grace You provide daily. Renew my spirit even as my outer self-shifts and ages. Let my marriage reflect Your faithfulness, not my perfection. And remind me that the work You began in me is still unfolding—beautifully, purposefully, and completely—until the day I see You face to face. Amen.*

# Epilogue


*Holly Wisdom for the Road Ahead*

If sixty years has taught me anything, it is this: God has never wasted a single chapter of my life. Not the tragic ones. Not the embarrassing ones. Not the sinful ones. Not the seasons where I did not recognize my own reflection in the mirror — physically or spiritually.

And sister, He will not waste yours either.

Everything you have read in this book has come out of lived theology — Scripture that has held me together, corrected me, confronted me, carried me, and kept me through the best and worst seasons of womanhood, marriage, motherhood, repentance, restoration, reinvention, and yes… menopause.

I am not the hero of this story. And although he is magnificent – my beloved isn't the hero either.

Christ is.

And this is what I want you to carry with you:

1. **God Has Carried You Every Step — and He Will Carry You Still**

   *"Even to your old age I am he, and to gray hairs I will carry you" (Is. 46:4).*

I look back at the years the locusts tried to eat — abuse, divorce, shame, trauma, aging, illness, grief, fear — and I see one truth: God carried me when I could not carry myself.

When I had nothing to offer but broken pieces, He held them together.

When I wandered, He followed.

When I ran, He stayed.

You are not too old, too damaged, too late, too tired, too changed, or too far gone for the God who knit you together (Psalm 139:13–14) and promised to finish the work He began in you (Philippians 1:6).

2. **Aging Is Not Losing Beauty — It Is Trading It for Wisdom**
   We fight gravity like it's a spiritual enemy. But the Bible calls aging a crown:

*"Gray hair is a crown of glory" (Pr. 16:31).*

Your body has changed — yes. Mine has too. But beauty in Scripture has never been about collagen or clothing; it has always been about character, reverence, peace, and the hidden person of the heart (1 Peter 3:3–4).

The world worships youth.

God crowns age.

The world rewards the visible.

God rewards the faithful.

3. **Your Marriage Is Still Holy Ground — Even When Life Shifts**

*"Two are better than one… a threefold cord is not quickly broken." — Ecclesiastes 4:9–12*

Marriage is not sustained by hormones, feelings, or perfect seasons. Marriage is sustained by covenant, grace, daily obedience, and by the Spirit of God who binds two sinners together in something sacred and supernatural. I have lived through the seasons where I felt unlovable, undesirable, ashamed, exhausted, sick, stretched thin, overwhelmed, and under-equipped.

But I have also lived through the miracles — the restoration only Christ could do. And here is the truth older Holly knows that younger Holly did not: Your husband does not see your insecurities — he sees his bride.

And God does not see your flaws — He sees Christ's righteousness.

### 4.   Scripture Is the Lifeline — Do not Drop It

If I survived these sixty years, it is because the Word of God became my oxygen.

When fear rose:

*"I sought the LORD, and he answered me and delivered me from all my fears" (Ps. 34:4).*

When shame screamed:

*"There is therefore now no condemnation for those who are in Christ Jesus." — Romans 8:1*

When my body failed me:

*"Though our outer self is wasting away, our inner self is being renewed day by day." — 2 Corinthians 4:16*

When I doubted my worth:

*"And her who was not beloved I will call 'beloved'" (Rom. 9:25)*

When I felt unseen:

*"You are the God who sees me." — Genesis 16:13*

When aging terrified me:

*"Strength and dignity are her clothing, and she laughs at the days to come." — Proverbs 31:25*

When intimacy felt fragile:

*"My beloved is mine and I am his." — Song of Solomon 2:16*

When life hurt:

*"The LORD sustains him on his sickbed." — Psalm 41:3*

When I didn't know how to go on:

*"The LORD is my strength and my song." — Psalm 118:14*

When I needed hope:

*"He restores my soul." — Psalm 23:3*

Scripture has never failed me.

And it will never fail you

5. **Laugh. Please. For the Love of All Menopausal Women — Laugh.**

God gave us humor because He knew we would need it.

The hot flashes, the disappearing hair, the increasing weight, the migrating backside, the vanishing metabolism, the confusion of "Is this holiness or hormones?"

None of this surprises Him.

None of this disqualifies you.

None of this makes you less of a woman or less of a wife.

Sister, He designed you with joy.

He designed you for laughter (Pr. 31:25).

He designed you to endure with grace and grit.

So laugh at the days to come.

They belong to Him anyway.

6. **The Gospel Is the Anchor Through Every Season**

   If I could give you one verse to tattoo on your soul, it is this:

   *"The LORD Himself will fight for you; you need only to be still."*
   *— Exodus 14:14*

I am sixty years old, and I can testify:

   God has fought for me more fiercely than I ever fought for myself.

   He fought for my healing.

   He fought for my marriage.

   He fought for my sanity.

   He fought for my identity (in Christ alone).

He fought for my joy.

He fought for my holiness (through Christ alone).

And He will fight for you.

7. **The Best Days Are Not Behind You — They Are Ahead**

Not because your body will magically return to its 25-year-old form (it will not).

Not because your marriage will suddenly become flawless (it will not).

Not because life gets easier (it does not).

But because Christ is making all things new (Revelation 21:5).

Even you.

Especially you.

Your story is still being written.

Your strength is still growing.

Your wisdom is still ripening.

Your faith is still deepening.

Your marriage is still sacred.

Your calling is still active.

Your soul is still blossoming.

And your God is still faithful.

**Final Blessing**

Sister, walk in joy.

Walk in truth.

Walk in grace.

Walk in courage.

Walk in Scripture.

Walk in laughter.

Walk in intimacy.

Walk in wisdom.

Walk in freedom.

Walk in Christ.

**And remember:**

You are fearfully made.

You are wonderfully held.

You are deeply loved.

You are not done yet.

*"Now to Him who is able to do far more abundantly than all that we ask or think... to Him be glory" (Eph. 3:20-21).* Amen, and amen.

# About The Author Holly T. Ashley, M. S.

◆◆◆

Holly T. Ashley is a writer, speaker, and curriculum developer known for her unapologetic, biblical approach to marriage, discipleship, and personal responsibility. With more than four decades of experience in domestic and sexual assault advocacy, she brings theological clarity, practical wisdom, and hard-earned honesty to topics often softened by culture. Holly is the co-founder and Executive Director of Cross Strength Ministries and holds a master's degree in forensic psychology. She develops Christ-centered resources focused on family restoration, biblical manhood and womanhood, and covenant faithfulness. She writes with conviction, humor, and grace—calling women to repentance, obedience, and joy rooted in God's design. Holly and her husband, David (MAA, MDiv), live just outside of Nashville, TN, and have four adult children and two grandchildren. They live out the truths they teach together in ministry and marriage.

I am my beloved's and he is mine

# About Cross Strength Ministries

*"True Strength is Found at the Foot of the Cross"*
*–Pastor David Ashley, MAA; MDiv (Founder)*

Cross Strength Ministries is a Christ-centered nonprofit dedicated to strengthening individuals, marriages, and families through biblical truth, personal responsibility, and disciplined discipleship. Founded on the conviction that real transformation comes through repentance, obedience, and grace, the ministry develops curriculum, classes, and resources addressing marriage restoration, parenting, biblical manhood and womanhood, domestic abuse awareness, and generational healing. Cross Strength Ministries confronts cultural distortions with Scripture, blending theological depth with practical application to equip believers to live ordered, faithful, and resilient lives—anchored in the gospel and strengthened for the long haul. For more information, books, and resources please go to CrossStrengthMinistries. org. To book Holly for your next women's ministry event contact us at info@CrossStrengthMinistries. org.